Savannah's Ghosts

by Al Cobb

Schiffer Publishing Ltd®

4880 Lower Valley Road, Atglen, PA 19310

Schiffer Books are available at special discounts for bulk purchases for sales promotions or premiums. Special editions, including personalized covers, corporate imprints, and excerpts can be created in large quantities for special needs. For more information contact the publisher:

Published by Schiffer Publishing Ltd.
4880 Lower Valley Road
Atglen, PA 19310
Phone: (610) 593-1777; Fax: (610) 593-2002
E-mail: Info@schifferbooks.com

For the largest selection of fine reference books on this and related subjects, please visit our web site at **www.schifferbooks.com**
We are always looking for people to write books on new and related subjects. If you have an idea for a book please contact us at the above address.

This book may be purchased from the publisher.
Include $5.00 for shipping.
Please try your bookstore first.
You may write for a free catalog.

In Europe, Schiffer books are distributed by
Bushwood Books
6 Marksbury Ave.
Kew Gardens
Surrey TW9 4JF England
Phone: 44 (0) 20 8392 8585; Fax: 44 (0) 20 8392 9876
E-mail: info@bushwoodbooks.co.uk
Website: www.bushwoodbooks.co.uk

Front cover photo by Sandra Mudge
Copyright © 2007 by Al Cobb
Library of Congress Control Number: 2006940064

ISBN: 978-0-7643-2701-8
Printed in China

Savannah's Ghosts

by Al Cobb

From Ghoulies

and Ghosties

Long Leggeties

Beasties

and Things that

Go Bump in the

Night

Good Lord Deliver Us.

FROM AN EARLY ENGLISH LITANY

Dedication

This book is dedicated to my mom who allowed me the freedom and security of a happy home when I was growing up even under occasional rocky situations. But *Life* is full of peaks and valleys that were designed to make us all stronger. I thank God I grew up in a country that gives us freedom of speech and freedom of the press and many other inalienable rights.

Thank you from the bottom of my heart, Florence Marion (Titus) Cobb.

Table of Contents

Preface

A Few Ghostly Updates
From the Desk of Al COBB

I have thoroughly enjoyed growing up in Savannah, Georgia, and raising my three children here. There are always so many interesting sights and activities to keep me occupied and investigating the supernatural in the coastal empire. The raw history surrounding each individual case leaves me with little time to keep up with the parade of old and new paranormal reports from the citizens of Savannah.

Since writing and publishing my first book entitled *Danny's Bed: A Tale of Ghosts and Poltergeists in Savannah, Georgia* (Whitaker Street Press), I have made many new friends and received a number of accounts of supernatural activities that took place in their homes and businesses. I may have opened the flood gates on ghost stories in Savannah both past and present when I came forward with my true adventure with poltergeists and communicating spirits. More than a few eyebrows were raised when I self-published my journal recently. More than four thousand copies sold in the region in the first few months, and I am very proud that my book was enjoyed by so many people. My first experience in publishing goes to prove you are never too old to achieve your dreams. I thank my lord Jesus Christ for all He did for my family and me. By calling upon His name, we have remained safe and our home is at peace.

When *Danny's Bed* was first released, our poltergeist story aired on the Fox Family network television series called *Real Scary Stories*. The making of a television pilot is a long and arduous task. Many hours went into the filming and very little ended up in the final program, but that's show biz. The show is a very short version of our tale, featuring my son Jason as the narrator. My wife Lila, Jason's twin brother Lee, and I have small roles telling the story about a small child's haunted antique oak bed that we purchased in September 1998 as a Christmas present for Jason.

No sooner had the bed been placed in Jason's room than things began to change from the norm. Jason had difficulty falling asleep and felt that he was under constant surveillance by something with eyes riveted on him.

Stranger still was the soft cool breath he felt at the nape of his neck, startling him from a light dream state into a rush of consciousness. The sudden pressing down on the mattress beside him by some invisible force confirmed an unknown presence lay beside him.

Strange as well was what happened to the photograph of Jason's recently deceased grandparents. He found it lying face down on the wicker lamp table near the headboard of the haunted bed. No matter how many times Jason would right the framed photograph, he, on return to his room, would find the photograph face down again. This scenario was repeated over and over. There was never a simple explanation to this mystery. Lila and I examined the back supports on the photo frame and found it stable. We checked to make sure that the table was level and no rush of air could be responsible from either the window or the air conditioner vent in the ceiling. The window was down and locked and the air was off, yet this framed photograph seemed to refuse the laws of physics and stand upright.

Jason first called Lila to his room to see if she could find out what was causing the unusual behavior of the framed photograph as well as his anxiety over sleeping in the bed. Jason and Lila experimented by righting the picture once again and then leaving the room and shutting the door behind them. They waited ten minutes then turned the brass doorknob and reentered Jason's room. They found the photograph down on its face yet again!

Later that same evening I returned from work and was relaxing in my easy chair when both Jason and Lila approached me and asked me to go downstairs with them to Jason's room. I complied and followed them halfway expecting some kind of joke to be played on me. My curious spirit got the best of me as I wondered what kind of net they would soon throw over the "old man."

We stood outside Jason's closed bedroom door when Lila turned to me and said in a hushed whisper, "Something very strange is happening here that neither Jason nor I can explain." I asked Lila what she meant and she proceeded to tell me what Jason and she had experienced. They both wanted me to witness the latest experiment they had going on.

As we opened the door and walked in, the photograph was down on its face again and had moved from one of Jason's lamp tables to the other! There were many more surprises ahead of us. Toys were laid out on top of Jason's bed, including some he had not played with since he was much younger. The closet door was partially open from where the toys were removed, and items next to his fish tank on his large mahogany dresser had been picked up and moved to the bed as well.

I could feel the presence of a child in the room as all three of us stood in the room dumbfounded by what we were seeing. I knew now that this was no joke and there wasn't any way in the world that this could be happening. I know that all access to the room was closed and locked, so teen trickery was 100% eliminated.

I felt strongly that a little male child presence was in front of me, so I called out to him: "Is your name Casper? Would you be six years old? Please tell us." I knew that if this spirit child had the ability to move toys around the room that he might have the capability to write down his name and age. I let "Casper" know that I had laid down a pencil and paper on the trunk at the foot of Jason's bed for him to write on.

We all stepped out into the hallway and shut Jason's door behind us. The brass knob made a gentle clicking noise. We waited outside the door and could hear movements in the closet and on the bed. Some kind of activity was taking place and time seemed to stand still for the ten minutes we gave the spirit to answer us. We did not want to rush in any sooner for fear of frightening him away.

The time had come. We gently knocked on the door to let the little spirit know we were coming in. The door pushed open and we all could see that the pencil and paper were lying as I had left them earlier, but underneath them was written "Danny 7"!

The adventures that Danny put my family and me through were enough to write a book about and I did. This experience led me to find others in my area who have an interest in the study of the supernatural and the paranormal.

While in mid–town Savannah one bright and cheerful Saturday morning on my weekly garage sale schedule, I stumbled across a sale held that day by a group called *The Searchers*.

The Searchers were founded in 1996 by Kathy Thomas and met in the beginning at the Media Play coffee house. Kathy is the Features Editor for *Creative Loafing Newspaper* in Savannah, Georgia. The club was formed to gather information and evidence of ghostly activity in and around Savannah. We meet bi-monthly and actively seek and study supernatural and paranormal events as they come to our attention. Our group researches and records all our findings for anyone wanting some answers to very difficult questions on hauntings in Savannah. We are strictly a non-profit group and not affiliated with any occult or Satanic group of any kind. We only wish to add to the knowledge of mankind and its purpose spiritually on this planet.

Currently, *The Searchers* are running ads in *Creative Loafing Newspaper* offering to help anyone who has a suspected haunting or other supernatural occurrence. The sheer number of incidences of ghosts and supernatural events led me to write this second book of eyewitness accounts and experiences gathered from people in all walks and stations of life in Savannah, Georgia. I hope "you all" will enjoy this *all-true* collection of *The Ghosts of Savannah, Georgia.*

Introduction

The ghosts of Savannah have been here since the first native Indians settled in southeast Georgia over 2500 years ago. The Creek Indian nation were the sole proprietors in the Savannah region and controlled the three major islands, St.Catherine's, Sapola, and Usabaw as well as the land track from Pipe Makers Creek to the boundaries of the town of Savannah and the surrounding lands.

The Creek Indian nation was divided into the Upper Creeks and the Lower Creeks. There were many tribal groups within the Creek nation. Among the prominent tribes in Savannah were the Yamacraw who signed peace treaties with the English settlers and became subjects of England. The treaty was signed on May 21, 1733. Tomo-Chi-Chi, Mico of the Yamacraw was instrumental in the negotiations and signing of the peace treaty which united the Creek Nation to the British Empire. Spain would have to think twice now before invading the coastal region of Georgia from their settlements in Florida.

The Creek Indians were well organized and lived bountifully off the deer, rabbit, raccoon, squirrel, possum and bear meat they hunted in the coastal forests. Corn and berries were favorite foods as well. To balance their diet, there was the Atlantic Ocean and Savannah River which provided all the fish, oysters, shrimp, and sea turtle the Creeks needed.

The Creeks also had a developed sense of the spiritual. They buried their dead in tombs with items that would help them in the afterlife, much like the ancient Egyptians. Shards of ancient Indian pottery is often found, including glass beads and arrow heads, in the multitude of burial mounds discovered in the South. And on St. Catherine's Island, archeological digs have brought forth evidence of Christian Indian burials. Skeletons discovered there have their arms crossed in the manner used in Spanish Catholic burial rituals. The Spanish had built missions on St Catherine's Island to educate the tribes and bring them the word of God, and a few gold crosses have been found on the island that date to the early seventeenth century. Archeologists are still gathering more information about the Indians who inhabited the islands off Savannah's coast. If you are standing in the center of a field that was once a Creek Indian village on the Georgia coast, it's easy to visualize in your mind their love of nature and this land. The Indian spirits are still making themselves evident to several eyewitnesses who have seen them at various times standing on the boating docks that now exist there. These spirits are wearing the same rawhide skins that their earthly counterparts wore in life. No one has ever been harmed by the Indian spirits spotted along these rivers and banks. The impression you feel is of a quiet Indian village with the women and children tending their cooking fires along the riverbank. I believe that they are still there living in the peaceful dimension of their hunting ground.

The first Europeans who settled on the Savannah River bluff, mainly adventurers, colonists, farmers, and merchants, brought tales of the supernatural based on the folklore of each settler's country of origin. Stories about ghosts, vampires, werewolves, and the "bogey man" were passed down from European storytellers. The entertainment in front of the fire on a cool winter's evening may well have been stories about the supernatural. People enjoyed the thrill of a scary story then as they do today.

One of the first casualties of these European settlers here was an English doctor named William Cox, who arrived on the Anne. The Anne was the ship, commanded by General Oglethorpe, that King George sent to colonize Georgia. If you're walking to 5 West York, there is a bronze wall plaque dedicated to him. The Georgia Historical Commission in 1967, dedicated this, the first colonial burial plot in Savannah. As more and more Georgians lived and died here, the small cemeteries grew larger and larger. Instead of a few isolated graves located on the bluff within sight of the Savannah River, they expanded to the Colonial Park Cemetery where thousands of the first Georgia colonists are buried. Many died in their youth. But whether they died from natural causes, the disastrous fires that gripped Savannah, or the Yellow Fever epidemics, Savannah's ghosts are here to stay, and many still wander Savannah today.

Ghosts and things that go bump in the night are not supposed to exist, yet more and more people are becoming convinced they do. Most people who have experienced a supernatural event in their lives will agree that most encounters begin in a perfectly innocent manner. It may be an item keeps disappearing and reappearing in a strange place. It could be a feeling of a presence. You may see a form or movement out of the corner of your eye. There are many variables possible. I will cover more on this topic in Chapter Three. Keep an open mind and a level head. Everyone has a certain psychic ability. It is as normal as our other five senses. We just don't use the ability or are not conscious that we use this ability that often. The ability is found deep within the brain. It is a part of our mind that is still a subject of intense study by psychologists. I leave many of these mysteries to the professionals.

The first contact isn't always scary or unsettling, but it can make you question your sanity until you have time to sort out the reality of the situation. As I gathered information on this project, I interviewed hundreds of local Savannahians from all walks of life. I interviewed real people with real stories of contact with the supernatural. This was exactly what I was searching for, and I didn't have to pry the information from anyone. They came to me with many fantastic stories, stories I have included in this volume.

At my very first book signing, a young couple walked up to me and showed me one of the most startling examples of ghost photography I have ever seen.The photograph they handed me was of several little girls standing in a bedroom with an amazing ghostly mist spread out like tentacles surrounding the girls and touching their upper bodies and heads as they played. A second picture showed a face looking out the same bedroom window as the little girl and her mom played out in the yard. There was no one in the house at the time the photograph was taken.

These photos were snapped during a normal sunny day, and no other abnormalities affected any other shots on the roll. The photographer did not notice anything strange as he took these shots. This happens quite a bit. In spirit photography unusual things show up all the time on film after it has been processed.

My first digital camera was a Sony 10X Mavica that I bought to record the paranormal poltergeist activities in my home. Most of the shots I took were in my home showing the messy state of our furnishings after each spectral visit. Everything was helter-skelter, with our bedroom curtains actually pulled off their rods to the floor and our blinds pulled up at cockeyed angles. Framed pictures were photographed turned at right angles and switched from room to room. To photograph an actual ghost is a very difficult thing to do, but it does happen and many times by pure accident. I have photographed spirit balls floating in several homes and back yards that I was investigating in Savannah. I have a couple of ghost photographs taken in downtown Savannah as well.

Most individuals who have seen ghosts catch them out of the corner of their eyes and then a split second later the apparition disappears into thin air. The best explanation for this is the fact that spirits are moving in our dimensional plane at such a velocity that they are invisible to us unless they choose to slow down and materialize before us. Catching a glimpse of a spirit on the fly like this is called spotting a fleeting apparition. Some ghost hunters have captured spirit images on video cameras. I have tried this myself and found that it can be very difficult. Several times when I left my camera on to film in my house it was manually turned off by the entity I was trying to film.

Another problem encountered was with the batteries I replaced in my digital camera and in the video cameras of fellow Searchers; with every replacement, the batteries would die in record time. These were brand new, unused multi-battery packs with full power capacity. These should have lasted hours, yet they didn't. Since ghosts are electromagnetic, batteries are like a piece of candy to them. Therefore when batteries fail under such conditions, it is often not the manufacturer's fault, but a sign of something more mysterious.

I welcome the resurgence of curiosity in things outside of the physical because it makes us think more profoundly of just what, ultimately, God's plan is for mankind. I find ghost research exhilarating. No doubt, as more and more people study and learn more about the metaphysical, it won't seem like some evil religion or occultist belief, but a natural progression of God's plan for us in the universe. I have always been fascinated and inspired to learn more about the Spirit of The Holy Ghost. In my research for this introduction, I opened up a copy of The King James Version of The Holy Bible to First Corinthians 12:7-13 which reads as follows: (7) But the manifestation of the spirit is given to every man to profit withal. (8) For to one is given by the spirit the word of wisdom; to another the word of knowledge by the same spirit; (9) To another faith by the same spirit; to another the gifts of healing by the same spirit; (10) To another the working of miracles; to another prophecy; to another discerning of spirits [to recognize or comprehend mentally]; to another divers kinds of tongues; to another the interpretation of tongues. (11) But all these worketh that one and the selfsame spirit, dividing to every man severally as he will. (12) For as the body is one, and hath many members, and all the members of that one body, being many, are one body: so also is Christ. (13) For by one Spirit are we all baptized into one body, whether we be Jews or Gentiles whether we be bond or free; and have been all made to drink into one Spirit.

I don't find it hard to believe in the Holy Spirit since I have personally seen him come alive within the hearts and minds of members of many churches I have visited in my life. Just as the air we breathe is invisible we can't deny that without it we would perish. We don't disbelieve that air exists just because we can't see it. So it is with the Holy Spirit who can inhabit the heart and soul of a being and make the most wonderful changes in a person that you could ever imagine.

The same spirits that existed since biblical times still exist today. Most of them are good and have no reason to harm man. They seem more bent on helping man get past all the problems he is dealing with while he is still a mortal on this Earth. I still maintain we should all keep an open mind but be cautious and weigh all the facts and information on any supernormal subject before coming to any conclusions. Hard evidence on ghosts and poltergeists is still very difficult to acquire, and frauds are still out there trying to make money and headlines about subjects they make up. The challenging implications and wide varieties of documented stories and accounts of supernatural activities is simply staggering. There is an ongoing study group in ghosts and poltergeists here in Savannah, Georgia, called The Searchers.I have been a member since 1998. There is no fee for our club's services and we are all happy to help anyone in the Savannah area with our knowledge of the supernatural. I really hope you enjoy this collection of stories and experiences from Savannah, Georgia.

--Albert L. Cobb Sr.

Biography

Albert L. Cobb, Sr.

I was born November 6, 1953, in Tulsa, Oklahoma, and, after graduating from Savannah Christian School here in Savannah in 1972, I began my first job a year later in the retail jewelry business at Desbouillions Jewelers. I studied the G.I.A. course on diamonds and colored stones under Frank Pruitt, store manager at the Medical Arts branch of Desbouillions Jewelers.

I married my high school sweetheart and fellow classmate Lila C. Cobb on July 3, 1974. We have three children. Our daughter, Jennifer Tara Cobb, was born in 1979 and was followed in 1984 by our twin sons, Albert L. Cobb Jr., whom we call Lee, and Jason Aaron Cobb. Desbouillions closed their downtown store in 1975 and I was among the employees caught in a company downsizing. I moved on to Segall and Sons Jewelers on White Bluff Road. Later, in 1980, I ran the Savannah Coin Shop.

In August, 1981, I opened Cobb's Gold and Silver Galleries on Derenne Avenue in Savannah. I incorporated and changed the name to Cobb's Galleries, Inc. in the mid 1980's. I am an appraiser of antiques and fine arts as well as most collectibles. I am a member of the American Art Pottery Association, and my firm is listed on Dunn and Bradstreet. I am called on by my customers and by insurance companies who need a competent appraiser.

This second collection of true ghost stories grew out of my love of investigating the supernatural. My hobbies used to be fishing, stamp collecting, metal detecting, coin collecting, and collecting television shows and movies, but, lately, investigating the paranormal with *The Searchers* has become an overriding interest.

THE SEARCHERS 2001

Front row l-r: Lee Cobb, Jason Cobb, Kaya Robinson, Sandra A. Mudge. Center l-r: Jourdan Calderon, Kathy Thomas, Lila Cobb, Al Cobb, Beth Ronberg, Ronda McCall. Back l-r: Bobbie Weyl, Jason Weyl, Alicia Willis, Danny Lamb, Billy Barret, Paul Ronberg, Mark Stevens.

Chapter One

The Ongoing Exploits of
the Searchers Paranormal Study Group

I am a member of a group of explorers involved in the study of the paranormal and unexplained activity in the city of Savannah, Georgia. Ghosts have always been fascinating to me ever since I first read in elementary school of their possible existence. My interest in ghosts and ghost stories has led me to feel it is conceivable that knowledge is passed on to the living through vivid dreams and, upon occasion, through physical contact.

The life force we all have can vary from one individual to another and from one circumstance to another. We are all born into this world with a purpose. It can be a learning experience or it can be for the purpose of reparation or inspiration to the cause of humanity.

The group I am in is called The Searchers. I joined it in November 1998 during a period in my life I have difficulty trying to explain. My family and I had our firsthand encounter with a young seven year-old spirit named "Danny" who happened to come with an antique bed that I purchased for my son Jason Cobb for a Christmas gift.

"Danny" would not allow Jason to have a comfortable rest on the bed, frequently pressing on the bed as Jason tried to sleep and moving toys all over the bed every time Jason left the room. "Danny" wrote a message to us that he had died in the bed in 1899 and did not want my son to sleep there.

I had read in a local newspaper called Creative Loafing of a local group of people in Savannah who studied paranormal reports from individuals in Chatham County and decided to contact them. I ran into them quite by accident (or fate) early one Saturday morning as I was making the rounds of garage sales that weekend.

The first person I spoke to was the club's founder Kathy Thomas. She and fellow member Danny Lamb were manning a booth selling an assortment of jewelry and other items to raise funds for The Searchers' activity fund. The other club members at the sale were as surprised as I was at the circumstances of our first meeting. They had all read in The Savannah Morning News of the Savannah man and his family's encounter with a poltergeist spirit named "Danny."

Kathy Thomas asked me if I would consider attending one of their Searcher meetings on an upcoming Friday night. I told her I would be happy to attend because I really needed to get some answers to the situation I was facing with "Danny" and the haunted bed in Jason's bedroom. I had talked just a few days prior to a Catholic priest because, from what I had seen on television and in the movies, I had been led to believe if something ultra-weird ever takes place, I should go directly to a Catholic priest. Priests, it seemed to me, would have a handle on anything paranormal and have the means to combat any evil attempting to enslave mankind.

Father M gave me a jar of crystal clear holy water which he blessed in front of me. He handed the container to me with instructions to sprinkle the contents on the bed, the walls, and the floor of the affected areas of Jason's bedroom. I brought the jar home with me that afternoon and followed the priest's instructions.

Holy water is great if you have an evil entity in your home. "Danny," however, was not impressed and the water did not exorcise him from Jason's room. Benign spirits are not distracted by holy water and it did not frighten "Danny" one iota.

During my first meeting with The Searchers I learned we all had much in common, and it felt more like a family gathering than a ghost hunting group. Meetings are held every two weeks at each member's home on an alternating basis. We each serve refreshments on the night it is our turn to host that week's meeting. Our mission is to try and study reports of ghostly phenomena that occur in our area. We gather information from each site we are called in to study. We then can authenticate whether a site is genuinely "haunted" by eliminating natural explanations. We use up-to-date scientific equipment to gauge the paranormal activities that are taking place at the reported site and document our findings in our Searcher Archives.

We often work in teams of four or more members when investigating a site to compare notes on each other's findings and preserve the integrity of each investigation. We are kept very busy by the ad we run in The Creative Loafing newspaper where Kathy Thomas is the Features editor. Many genuinely concerned individuals have contacted The Searchers with stories of the bizarre and the unusual for our group to investigate.

This past year alone we have investigated many historical and modern sites about which the owners and tenants alike have told us stories of their personal experiences that would make your skin crawl. Stories of seeing fleeting spirits from the corner of their eyes in both daylight and darkness tell of twenty-four hour activity of these entities.

We also have made visits to local cemeteries of which Savannah is famous. None of us would ever be without our trusted high speed cameras, recorders, video cameras, and other important scientific equipment. We have been very successful photographing Spirit Balls of light, and the dark shadows of fleeing specters trying hard not to be caught on camera. We can't always explain many of the strange photos of the supernatural we have taken, but we take great care not to represent a photo as authentic till we have eliminated possible natural causes of each photograph.

We spent the night in the newly restored Marshall House by special request of the hotel's management prior to its grand opening. They had reports and observations of paranormal activity and called Kathy Thomas about our group doing an on-site and overnight investigation. We were thrilled at the opportunity and were given the entire second floor with access to all areas from the basement to the roof.

During the Civil War the Marshall House had been used as a Union hospital, and many troops were operated on (and many died there) during the occupation of Savannah in 1864-65. A number of hotel employees have seen and heard a phantom tabby cat, the ghost of a little girl, and a Union officer walking the long, narrow hallways of the Marshall House.

Without a doubt our group of five teams found a healthy dose of paranormal activity all around us from the moment we entered the hotel lobby. My family and I comprised one team and we heard the phantom tabby cat make a loud scream in the basement, and my son Jason saw the cat move through the wall downstairs. The basement was found to contain tons of black ash and other sediment and under it were the human remains comprised of, we believe, partial skeletons of Civil War patients.

When we first arrived, I took a number of photos of the hotel's lobby and long narrow hallways. I found a large number of active Spirit Balls from the floor to the ceiling and floating around the night manager and several members of our group. Spirit Balls are a sure sign of active entities present at the site you may be investigating.

Two groups of Searchers placed recorders near rooms and stairwells where sightings and/or paranormal experiences were taking place as reported by both hotel employees and sensitive members of our group. Both recorders captured unexplained garbled talking sounds and one tape had a heavy footstep followed by an obvious dragging sound.

We are always happy to greet new members to our ranks. Our regulars come from many religions and walks of life. We are not a coven or a religious clique. We are simply everyday folks who have a strong interest in the paranormal and all the facets found in the mysterious and unexplainable. Our group is comprised of teachers, psychologists, photographers, realtors, housewives, retailers, students, appraisers, tour guides, and petting zoo owners, to name just a few.

We only ask each person who would like to join us to be friendly and open minded to all the experiences and knowledge that God lays out for mankind in the universe. As I mentioned earlier, we do have members within our ranks who are highly perceptive to sights and sounds most of us do not hear. They are sensitive to and can come in tune with the history of any given site we visit. They feel a pulse that could be the remnant of an occurrence that may have taken place at that spot a hundred years before or a current registration of paranormal activity. Sometimes they are impressed by a mental vision that plays back an event much like a spool of film playing at your local theatre. The sensitive can act like a psychic and often help make contact with the spirit entity(s) causing the investigation to take place. Many of the successful conclusions to our paranormal investigations I credit to those in our group who feel and communicate with the spirits or who can answer if we are dealing with a true spirit or not. We all work well together and have gotten along since I joined The Searchers. I find that helping others with their ghosts or poltergeist experiences is very exhilarating and rewarding. At this time The Searchers does not charge for its help and consider it an honor to give insight on each paranormal circumstance it encounters. Don't be afraid to contact cobbsinc@aol.com" or fax me at 1-912-233-2827. My office number is 1-912-234-1582.

If you are interested in joining an international group of ghost hunters and researchers, you may wish to contact The American Ghost Society. It has over 500 members in the United States and Canada. Founded in 1996 by Troy and Amy Taylor, it can be contacted on the web at http:// HYPERLINK "http://www.prairie ghosts.com" www.prairie ghosts.com or be reached by telephone at 1-888-446-7859.

The American Ghost Society is seeking genuine evidence that is thoroughly analyzed and authenticated before presenting the findings to the general public. By carefully examining all the facts of each investigation, the group protects the integrity of the truth and nothing but the truth. This policy protects the American Ghost Society's good name from ever being compromised. Its members do not use psychics or conduct metaphysical experiments in their research. They will use assistance through other sources when a case does prove to be genuine and only by the location owner's request. It is also very important that they do not claim to be experts in the paranormal or the supernatural. I know of no experts in the field and have dealt with two world-renown and extremely knowledgeable parapsychologists: Dr. William Roll and Dr. Andrew Nichols. Both of these esteemed gentlemen are tops in their field and are called by government and private sources to investigate paranormal occurrences throughout the world. The American Ghost Society works hard to present the image of the ghost researcher as a competent individual collecting authentic evidence in proving the existence of entities outside of the norm. People jokingly call paranormal researchers "ghost busters" after the movie of the same name. In reality, we are just plain folk on a mission to discover and uncover mysteries, myths, and truths that have stumped mankind for thousands of years. Contact The American Ghost Society, and it can offer you a membership packet containing all you need to become a ghost hunter or researcher in your home town.

Tour buses and tour guides ply their trade daily in historic Savannah, Georgia.

Beautiful azaleas in full bloom make a visit to Savannah in the spring – a lifetime memory.

Chapter Two

First Hand Accounts of
Tour Guides in Savannah Meeting Spirits

In the Beautiful city Savannah, Georgia, home of many tour companies and expert guides in the history of the region, many people have had encounters with ghosts, and unexplainable phenomena. I spoke with several tour guides who have had bizarre and surreal experiences while in the process of giving lectures to their clients while on foot in local cemeteries and around native burial grounds.

Several told me that even while parked outside Colonial Cemetery they felt extreme changes in temperature inside their vehicles and upon entering the grounds they could feel the energy of other entities around them. One tour guide admitted she felt her ears fill up and could not hear for a few brief moments. She said as soon as she regained her hearing she could feel the presence of someone sitting behind her, although she had earlier dropped off the last couple on the tour. Later, that same evening, as she parked the long trolley and drove home in her own car, the presence followed her into her mid-town home. At this point, the screen door opened on its own accord.

After preparing dinner for her large family, she sat in front of her television watching a favorite program when the television switched itself off. She did not understand how this happened so she cut the set back on only to have it repeat the act. The following day when she returned home the television set was blaring. No one was home yet, and she clearly remembered turning the set off while heading to work uptown. This incident happened several times until she felt the presence leave and go back with her to her job on the tour trolley. Once again she felt the presence leave as she dropped off her uninvited passenger back to its home in the cemetery.

When speaking with tour guide Mitchell Mayer at my office on a cloudy December afternoon, we discussed incidents he was keenly aware of during his "haunted" walking tours. On a recent tour with a group of men, women, and children Mitchell walked into Colonial Cemetery and as he spoke about the various tombstones and their histories. At the south end of the grounds, several spectators within his group noticed a patch of fog hovering over three graves that lay side by side. No fog was evident over any other grave of the cemetery grounds that rainy night. The fog hovered over this one specific area near the gravestones. It was odd and curious and as Mitchell wound up his lecture and the group turned to leave the cemetery, the mysterious fog lifted and disappeared.

Mitchell then turned back to his clients and asked them if they had ever heard of taking home a ghost with them. The moon shone through the cloudy night sky. "Sometimes, when you take a ghost tour in Savannah, you get much more than you bargained for," he coolly said. Twice, while touring in front of the Davenport House and The Keehoe House, Mitchell had young girls in his charge stare and point upward to the high attic windows and exclaim they saw a little girl in a white dress look through the window at them and smile. Even before he could relate the tragic tale of a little girl in a white dress that had died there in the nineteenth-century, they had beat him to the punch by seeing her upstairs!

On a more personal note, several of my friends have had similar paranormal experiences. Beth Ronberg and her husband Paul are a case in point, having both had a number of paranormal experiences in the past. Paul is a computer technician with a prominent South Eastern oil company, and Beth has a fine petting zoo business called Critters-To-Go in Savannah. Beth also is involved in the tour guide business and is well aware of the haunted side of Savannah, Georgia.

Beth has graciously supplied her own account of a very interesting story involving the supernatural on her personal walking tours through the streets, parks, and cemeteries of historic Savannah, Georgia. The following statements are from Beth Ronberg and I have included her own account in Ghosts in Savannah. So, take it away, Beth:

It has become quite obvious to me, as a tour guide of Savannah's historic district, specializing in Ghost Tours, that we as a city like to flaunt our ghosts. Savannah is currently ranked as one of the top three most haunted cities in America, due mostly to its destructive and often heinous past, and it is no wonder the spirits still dwell among us.

Savannah's architecture has been wonderfully preserved in a great many renovated structures, which still boast some original occupants. Ghosts, spirits, specters, apparitions, they are called by many names, but actually are not all that diverse in their nature.

There are several different types of hauntings that are common to areas such as Savannah. Most of the events reported in supposedly haunted houses have to do with imprints, or visions of the past. Somehow, tragic and emotional events have a way of recording themselves on structures, or in the atmosphere where these events occurred. However, there are those spirits that are actually conscious of our presence and choose to interact in our world.

I feel that those are the spirits that I and/or my patrons have actually encountered during some of my tours. Visits such as these are rare but have definitely occurred.

Encounters with spirits can occur via any one of our five senses. Most times people do not actually See a ghost with their eyes, but experience an apparition in some other subtle way. I have had many different types of people on my tours, from the classic skeptic that chose to take the tour for the fun of it, to those who are truly interested in the paranormal side of life. Generally, my tours are geared to the overall age of the group. Most of my patrons are Girl Scouts visiting the birthplace of Juliette Gordon Lowe, founder of the Girl Scouts. Since I usually cater to the scouts on these tours, the chaperones are left to their own conclusions.

Most of them can't determine if I am just telling stories for the sake of the girls, but they usually understand before the conclusion of the tour that I have a little more than a general understanding of the ghostly activity in the area.

I usually begin a tour by trying to allay any fears from the younger clients. I then proceed to take the group on a set route throughout the historic district, where some of the more famous stories of haunted happenings are recorded. However, many times I will vary my route to include sites that I find historically fascinating, and that are also known for their supernatural activity. It is at these times that I include stories of The Searchers' paranormal investigations of certain areas or buildings. This is when I get the most questions about my unusual hobby, but I find that the adults are particularly fascinated by my true legends, and usually are willing to confide in me some of their own personal experiences with the paranormal.

One of my favorite haunts is the Colonial Park Cemetery. Historically, it is one of the most interesting areas in Savannah. My tours usually end midpoint at the cemetery, where we can spend a fair amount of time just talking history. One of the key facts regarding this particular cemetery is that it was heavily vandalized during the Civil War. The majority of headstones are missing, and quite a number of them have been altered, supposedly by the many soldiers that camped out there for the several months that General Sherman's troops occupied the city.

It is these stones that have been modified that I like to talk about. Most of the altered headstones have easily detected changes, such as added digits to the deceased persons age, etc. However, one particular stone that I like to point out is one that has three distinct changes that are not easily discernable. The stone lays toward the front part of the cemetery, and lays flat, just off the main path. Underneath this stone lie the remains of Frederick and Ursula Herb, and it is one that was originally carved from white marble. It is in excellent shape, compared to the majority of the stones throughout the cemetery that have weathered badly over the decades. You have to read the entire epitaph several times to notice the mistakes. The dates for Ursula Herb have been altered. Specifically, the stone currently reads that Ursula Herb was born in the year 1711, and died in the year 1811, yet the very next line says she was 73 years old. When the gravesite was originally pointed out to me, it was thought that Ursula's age was changed, and in fact that she died at 100 years old. However, back in the 19th century, it was uncommon for people to live even into their sixties, so I reviewed the stone up close and noticed that the year 1711 had been changed from the true date, 1741 and that the death date of 1811 had in fact been 1814, which, after doing some quick math, added up to 73 years of age.

The changes were cleverly made, and I can only guess at the method used to fill in the 4's to make them 1's, but I could easily see that those who changed this stone took some time and care in their work. The other change on the stone is in Frederick's date of birth. The date currently reads that Frederick was born on March 1th. In fact this is another 4 that has been altered to look like a 1. I have a lot of fun with my patrons on tour, having them try to pick out the mistakes in this stone.

Up until the summer of 2000, it was common for walking tours to visit the Colonial Park Cemetery in the evening. Usually several tour groups would wind up in the same area at the same time, so guides would respect each other and migrate to different sections of the cemetery, so that their groups would not be disturbed by others. My spot was towards the middle of the cemetery. I would usually have my patrons sit on one of the low monuments facing the cemetery entrance and the main path, and tell my customary historical facts. Regardless of what type of group I had (usually Girl Scouts), I would always talk about the soldiers vandalizing the cemetery, and end my time by pointing out the stone of Frederick and Ursula on our way out of the park. Unfortunately, about January of 2000, the second lamppost along the main path had a burned out light bulb. You will recall this is where Frederick and Ursula's stone lay. The first time I noticed this, I realized how difficult it was to read this stone without it being lit up, but I did my best. It turns out that this particular light was burned out for several months, and I always had a hard time showing people this particular stone.

One night in mid-March, I had a rather large Girl Scout group on tour. We were having a great time, and arrived at Colonial Park just after dark. Of course, the first thing I noticed was that the second lamppost light was still burned out. Ignoring this (since I was used to improvising by this time), I took my group to our familiar spot and started my stories. For some reason, this group was rather eager and enthusiastic, more so than usual, and the subject of history never came to light, but rather we were talking about supernatural happenings occurring throughout Savannah. I try to keep our time in the cemetery limited, because I tend to get carried away, and could possibly spend most of the night there if given the chance. I realized that I was taking a lot of time on this tour, and had not at this point mentioned any of the vandalism that took place during the Civil War. Therefore, I made the decision to forego that aspect of the history, and therefore not make my usual pit stop at the Herb's gravesite. As I turned toward the main entrance to lead my group out, I immediately noticed that the second lamppost light, (that 10 minutes previously was not lit) was definitely alight. Now, I decided that I wouldn't mention this fact to anyone, since no one would understand without a lengthy explanation, but made another hasty decision and took this opportunity to take my group to Frederick's and Ursula's site, and talk about the vandalism. Of course this lengthened my tour another ten minutes, but I felt obligated, so to speak. After this segment of my tour was complete, I turned my group once again toward the entrance to the cemetery. Since it was a rather large group, as I approached the front gates, I turned myself around to make sure the entire group was still with me. At this point, another most bizarre phenomena occurred. The second lamppost, which now was lit like a Christmas tree, dimmed and extinguished itself, right before my eyes! Up to this evening, I personally had not had any paranormal experience this blatant occur to me. I therefore had to relay this entire experience to my group, since they were indeed witness to it too. My feeling is that Frederick and Ursula's spirits were so used to me talking about them, that they couldn't allow me to depart the cemetery, even this once, without a mention. Beth Ronberg 2001

All of Savannah's tour guides try to give their patrons the experience of a lifetime. There are hundreds of supernatural stories being told on a daily basis to tourists while on the ghost tours. Some stories are simply amazing and sound far fetched, but since fact is stranger than fiction, why bother to make anything up?

Chapter Three

How To Know If Your
Home Is Haunted or Not

Seventy percent of "hauntings" can be explained by normal means. Water heaters and air conditioners running their normal cycles can leave the uninitiated with the impression that something is walking around in the attic or basement. If you are not used to hearing certain sounds such as the wind howling or a branch scraping the roof of your home, it can give you a case of the willies. Ice machines and refrigerators generate a lot of noises to the jumpy souls out there who happen to be spending a quiet evening at home reading or listening to music. Most people are familiar with the sounds of their house settling, whether old or new. The human mind can play tricks on a person, and all these sounds combined with an overactive imagination can make the bravest person paranoid. If your lights flicker on and off, it is a sign that the life of the light bulbs are nearing their end and not necessarily a reason to call 911 for a parapsychologist.

If you eliminate these possible causes, you will then be on the right trail to determine if you have a legitimate haunting in your home or not. It is the other thirty percent of unexplainable phenomena that makes ghost hunting so exciting and rewarding. It is great to help someone alleviate their fears of the unknown. You can often help the haunting entity find his or her way into the light as well. Below are some tips on telling if your house is haunted or not. There can be a combination of paranormal incidents so be alert to any or all of them.

- *Something touches your arm, legs, or hair.*
- *A powerful feeling of being watched overwhelms you*
- *Electrical appliances turn off and on without human intervention*
- *Severe temperature changes of unexplained origin*
- *Water faucets and toilets operate without human intervention*
- *Light to heavy pad of footsteps are heard when no one is there*
- *Music coming from unexplained sources*
- *Distinct odors of perfumes, cigars, or other less palatable smells*
- *Banging, tapping, or knocking sounds in the walls*

- *Missing personal items that keep turning up in the oddest places*
- *Pictures switched or turned at right or left angles*
- *If your home appears to look like the aftermath of a burglary*
- *If you experience the sighting of a white/grayish object floating through a wall in your home*
- *If your family photographs contain orbs of light that are not reflections taken in your home*
- *If small children visiting your home claim to see someone you can't*
- *If lamp shades are removed from lamps without human intervention*
- *If your telephone calls are interfered with by strange static or cut off entirely*
- *If you are directly communicated with through disembodied voices or actual written messages on notes or scratched on the wall*

These are the most common activities pointing to a haunting as reported in many firsthand accounts I have researched. Even if you qualify for several of these, you must also allow for teen trickery or the possibility of a living individual trying to drive you away from your home for reasons of his or her own. Check and double check all the resources at your disposal. If all other attempts have failed to find a reason to all this insanity, the best thing you can do is find the nearest expert on the paranormal.

My first contact was a Catholic priest who listened to my story and offered me a bottle of holy water to spread throughout my home. He seemed used to being approached by people with similar problems. He offered to bless my home in case the holy water had no effect on the entities that haunted our domicile. You can talk to close friends and ask their opinions or contact shop owners who specialize in items related to the occult and ask them if a psychic circle group exists in your area and seek their help.

Take out your city directory and make a few inquiring phone calls to Psychics and Mediums listed in the Yellow Pages. Parapsychologists are a little tougher to find but you can receive help in contacting them through colleges and universities having a Psychology department. If you are still looking for help, go to a bookstore and look for books in the "New Age" section and write or call people who have written true accounts on the supernatural. I have learned that thousands of people have had some kind of unexplainable event take place in their lives.

In Savannah, Georgia, the locals have thousands of ghost stories that will make anyone's hair stand on end. When I related my story of the haunted bed to my friends and acquaintances, they told me they experienced goose bumps. When I ended my talk of my experiences, they agreed that similar things had caused concern to them or a close relative. Savannah is the most haunted city in the United States as stated on The History Channel in a recent TV program called "Haunted Savannah.After you have discovered whether your home is haunted or not, you should be able to achieve peace of mind. Ninety-nine point nine percent of spirits are benign and only wish us to acknowledge their co-existence in our homes. Many Savannahians who know they have a ghost in their home are comfortable having it stay. As long as both parties observe each other's boundaries, the ghosts are never lonely and their hosts never worry about a lack of conversation at social events. If you ever have to go one-on-one with a ghost, just remember that you are in control of your home. This is your life and this is your time on Earth. Simply order any offending spirit out of your home by commanding that in the name of Jesus Christ, you wish it to leave. Say the Lord's prayer as well and the spirit will be forced to leave your presence. Sometimes it will return momentarily for one last time. Just repeat your command in the name of Jesus Christ and it will leave. Most ghosts are not dangerous and are only restless and unhappy. We can choose to live with them, get rid of them, or simply ignore them. Most people choose the latter and I fully understand their reasons why. I have found that the largest majority of people I know are open minded about ghosts and spirits in our new age. I cannot stress to you enough to read and learn all you can about spirits through the Holy Bible and books on ghosts that have recently been published to gain knowledge on the subject. The worst fear that man can have is the fear of the unknown.

Photo by Kathy Thomas

Chapter Four

The Spectre in Paradise Park

B illy Ray Hensley and his wife Ruby Nell were good friends of mine
whom I met at yard sales and auctions in Savannah many years ago.
We used to go head-to-head every Friday and Saturday morning in the wee
hours at garage and tag sales. We had a mutual appreciation of each other's
talent for getting out of bed early and searching out the best finds of the
weekend. We were "friendly competitors" as I like to refer to my yard sale
adversaries.

Ruby was always in search of toys and educational things for all her
grandchildren and nephews and nieces. Billy Ray bought furniture and collectibles to resell and to give away. It was always a real challenge to race
with them each and every weekend for the few treasures left out at yard
sales these days. Ever since the advent of The Antiques Road Show and the
British version of the Antiques Road Show in the mid 1990's pickings have
gotten slimmer and slimmer. Now everyone thinks they own the crown
jewels and are fearful of giving anything away at a yard sale. It has made
the job much harder to locate an item that can be sold to pay for the gas it
takes to seek it out.

One Saturday morning while Billy Ray and I were waiting for an estate
sale to open, he recounted a tale to me that had taken place several times at
his home on Regent Drive in Paradise Park. He told me that both he and
Ruby had seen the woman who once owned their home on several occasions. She had died several years before and they had never met her in real
life and had no idea what she looked like. When telling their neighbors
what they thought they saw, they were told the description fit the previous
owner to a "T."

Billy Ray explained to me that when he would be relaxing in his chair
the family pet would suddenly stand and point at the doorway. Animals
seem to have a second sight when it comes to seeing and feeling invisible
entities. The dogs fur would stand on end and Billy Ray could feel a cold
chill as if someone put cold hands on his arm. Goose bumps would rise on

Billy's skin and stay there till the entity left the room, as quietly as she came in. The dog would then return to normal as if nothing had happened. Ruby too had similar experiences but she caught images of the woman doing housework out of the corner of her eyes.

Both Billy Ray and Ruby Nell Hensley were killed in a tragic automobile accident in Statesboro, Georgia, recently. Someone ran a stop sign at highways 46 and 67 in Bulloch County. They will both be missed by friends and family alike. I sometimes have the feeling they are ahead of me as I approach my next garage sale. We all had fun going to sales every week and I get the feeling they still do as well.

Photo by Sandy Mudge

Chapter Five

Fleeting Apparitions Seen
at the Super 8 Motel

Since the Super 8 Motel opened fifteen years ago at I-95 and 204, there have been reported sightings of the spirits of a woman and a man wandering the narrow hallways and appearing out of nowhere in plain view of employees on duty at the front desk. The Lady in White first appeared to Amy Morton in 1996 when she was on duty in the motel's reception area. The office is equipped with an alarm on the door which continues to go off by itself whenever Amy is alone. The strong smell of rose water is prevalent to the point of giving Amy headaches. The feeling of being watched and followed is made more real by doors opening and shutting on their own within a few feet of her.

On one occasion, Amy looked up from her bookwork and spotted the Lady in White staring down at her from the top of the stairs. She was semi-translucent in a stark, white high-collared dress typical of the sort popular in the teens to early 1920's. The form disappeared as quickly as she appeared when Amy tried to focus her eyes but she has since reappeared many times to Amy. The Lady in White has also been seen by other female employees of the Super 8 Motel. An ex-employee named Jennifer was actually the first to see the Lady in White and report it to her room mate Amy. Both Amy and Jennifer seem to be very sensitive to spirit contact. Amy told me that even as a small child growing up in Springfield, Missouri, she had seen a spirit form of a mysterious man watching her from her doorway.

The Lady in White has appeared to still others working at the Super 8. Two housekeepers, Audrey Fraser and Linda Sherman have both seen The Lady in White out of the corner of their eyes. She appeared with long brown hair in the same white dress and seemed to float near the staircase or by the doorway. She materializes in three separate ways: a full three-dimensional look, a partial semi-translucent look, and a shadow-like look. The energy level output of the spirit determines how well we can perceive it in our dimension. So far, no guests staying at the Super 8 have seen the spirits flitting about, and only female employees are affected. The second spirit seen by the ladies at the Super 8 Motel is a white male spirit appearing to be in his mid to late 20's, dressed in black pants and a red flannel shirt. He always carries with him an axe or a hatchet. He loves to sneak up on the ladies and peer around corners staring straight at them and scaring the B' Jesus out of them. He has appeared in a semi-translucent form to both Amy and Jennifer. Amy recounted a story that while she and Jennifer were on duty the spirit they call Big Red followed them around until they were so frightened they ran outside the motel. Amy tells me that since Jennifer has left the company Big Red has not returned either.

The current manager of the Super 8 Motel, Denise Stagpool, told me that while she believes in the spirit world she would rather not experience the same things her employees have seen. She hasn't yet seen the fleeting apparitions. She did say that while working on a night audit into the wee hours of the morning she experienced a heavy change in the atmosphere in her office at 3:13 A.M. that forced her out of the building so she could breathe. She described her experience as extremely frightening, and she felt she had to get fresh air or die.

There is definitely a connection to the women who work at the Super 8 Motel, and the psychic impressions they have all been feeling relating to the spirits residing there. There are many case histories of women being more sensitive than men when it relates to the human mind. It may not be very long before a sensitive male checks in and meets the spirits of the Super 8 Motel.

Photo by Sandy Mudge

Chapter Six

Please, Lady, Come Back! Come Back!

There are occasions in this world that spirits become entangled in unfinished business and fail to go into the light of heaven. Either death came without warning and there was no time to make amends with the Lord or the spirit chose not to go into the light for a myriad of reasons. Mortals rarely are able to know the exact time of their deaths with the exception of prisoners on death row or military soldiers in heated battle. Even then, the Governor may pardon a prisoner in the eleventh hour or, for the soldier, the heated battle may end as quickly as it began.

This is referred to as being *stuck* in our plane of existence. The spirit's consciousness of himself or herself does not fully comprehend that death has come. Many spirits stay behind thinking they will meet up with individuals they steered clear of in this life and do not want to meet them again in the next realm. Some stay behind to help grieving friends and family overcome their sadness or to watch their children grow or to tend to family interests from beyond the grave. There are hundreds of case histories involving the return of loved ones saying a final farewell or guiding a family to a important document or will that has been hidden or buried in a secret location.

Murder victims' spirits will stay behind in order for their killers to be found and justice to be served. Then, they move on into the light. Some spirits are very comfortable here in the earthly plane and even though they are given the green light to pass over into the *white light* they choose not to. This is one of many reasons to be prepared mentally no matter what religion you have chosen to meet your Creator at the end of your lifetime here on Earth.

Laurel Grove Cemetery was the site of one of the most exciting encounters our group *The Searchers* has ever experienced. It was a cool, moonlit evening when we met Colin Young at the gates of Savannah's second oldest cemetery. We had made arrangements for our group to take a lantern tour by one of Savannah's most prominent cemetery historians and tour guides. The cemetery had closed two hours earlier and shadows had darkened into pitch blackness. Our cars lined the dark narrow roadway as we proceeded to grab our flashlights and lanterns and follow Colin into the wide maw of the cemetery gates. As soon as we were inside, he and his helpers closed and locked them behind us for security reasons.

Colin would stop from time to time and give us background on many of the important Georgians buried there. It was truly an enjoyable and fascinating excursion into history and I highly recommend it to everyone visiting Savannah, Georgia. It wasn't long before our group encountered a special area called *The Gettysburg Section* populated by rows of Civil War soldiers buried there from both the Confederacy and the Union .

Some of our member's are very sensitive to the communications these lonely spirits can relay. Sometimes, it is a mental impression that is so strong that thoughts are received in the form of mental telepathy. Such was the case of one of our members, Bobby Weyl, the very moment after setting foot in this hallowed ground just inside of the perimeter of *The Gettysburg Section*. Bobby was being called to from the left and right by the spirits of these brave Civil War soldiers who died so young.

They all seemed to be vying for her attention at the same time. Voices rang out to her and caused an intense feeling of sadness. She was visibly upset and felt as if all her strength was leaving her. She envisioned a Confederate officer who walked toward her and introduced himself as James Johns and next to him stood a young man about seventeen-years old. The young man told her he had left his home on the farm for the grand adventure of fighting the Yanks. Instead he met with his death. The voice of the southern farm boy sounded to Bobbie's ears like it was coming from a deep well in the ground. Bobby began to see through the eyes of the young Confederate as his unit fought in hand-to-hand combat. She watched the battle as if it were being reenacted on *The History Channel.* The final scene was the high pitched scream of the boy as a bayonet was thrust into his chest. He fell to the ground in a heap with many other dead and mortally wounded troops. No one came to tend his wounds and he slowly and painfully bled to death. Bobbie felt her legs buckle under her and was dizzy and crying and extremely upset. She was led away from the site by our esteemed club founder, Kathy Thomas. Bobby kept hearing over and over the spirit calling out, "Lady, Come Back! Please, Come Back!" as Kathy led her around *The Gettysburg Section.*

Meanwhile, my son Jason Cobb and I were walking at the forefront of the remaining members of our group. Jason pointed to a row of tombstones some yards ahead of us and told me he knew that we would find a grave marked *Cobb.* The night was pitch black and Jason had never been to this cemetery before so I asked him how he could be so sure. He said he just knew. I aimed the flashlight off to the left as he directed me and we found the grave of a Confederate private named *J.A .Cobb*! The very same initials as my son's *Jason Aaron Cobb*! It may just be a coincidence, but I feel the energy we all experienced in the cemetery that night was phenomenal.

We finished our site tour that night and returned to our homes. When Bobby arrived home from *The Searcher's* lantern tour she was still shaking from her ghastly experience. She was in her kitchen fixing a late night snack in the microwave when she found herself singing a Civil War song called *Annabelle Leigh*. She found the words and the tune flowing from her lips as if she had sung the tune her whole life. This could have been a recollection of a tune imprinted from one of the Civil War soldiers in contact with Bobby that dark Friday night at *Laurel Grove Cemetery*.

We should all take the time to visit our local cemeteries and "commune with the dead." As their descendents we have the power to pray for those past, present, and future . We must let them know we are proud of them and the accomplishments they made while in this life. We have the power to console those who, for whatever reason, have not crossed over, and we can help them go into *God's White Light!*

Hampton Lillibridge House

Chapter Seven

Jim Williams 1964 Interview on the Haunting at the Hampton Lillibridge House on St. Julian St. in Savannah

One of the few remaining eighteenth-century homes in Savannah is located on 507 East St. Julian Street. The house was built over 200 years ago by a Rhode Islander named Hampton Lillibridge who found the warm climate in Savannah and Sea Island Georgia suitable for a home and a plantation. The beautiful four-story home with its high gambrel roof is topped off with a widow's walk like typical homes in New England along the seacoast. Over 400 homes were burned to the ground in the fire of 1820, but the Hampton Lillibridge house survived.

Some years later Hampton died and his widow married a gentleman named Joseph Grant. They lived there for a few years longer and sold the home for $25,000 to another New Englander who also owned a plantation at Sea Island named James Gould. In 1963, Savannah decorator and antiques dealer Jim Williams purchased the Hampton Lillibridge house, which was by now vacant and in dire need of restoration. He moved it from its old location from East Bryan Street and began to gather the workers and supplies for the massive project.

Beginning in the mid-1950s, the restoration movement began in earnest. The Davenport House was among the first that was saved and restored. Jim Williams was a man with great foresight and bought and restored over 50 homes in his lifetime. He was inspiring to other Savannahians to rebuild or restore many historical buildings in our fair city. There were many problems Jim Williams encountered from the beginning in his dealings with The Hampton Lillibridge house. The first incident occurred when the house beside the Hampton Lillibridge collapsed tragically killing a workman who was helping move the house for Jim. Although the house had stood vacant for years before Jim Williams rescued it from the wrecking ball, it had a very checkered history of anger and violence from the past when it had been a rooming house for sailors and transients. One story tells us that in one of the upstairs bedrooms a sailor had hung himself from a knob of the bed's high brass headboard. The dramatic change in the location of the house may well have awakened the spirits in the Hampton Lillibridge and began what paranormal investigators call Savannah's most haunted house.

My good friend Burl Womack, a well known and greatly admired radio talk show host, interviewed Jim Williams on October 31, 1964, for a radio show on NBC broadcast nationally. Burl is best known for his morning drive show called "Breakfast with Burl." Every morning Savannahians would wake up to Burl's deep booming voice telling us how much he was enjoying his Krispy-Kreme donuts as he poured steaming hot coffee into his china mug. The show's hook was the microphones picking up every sound of his donut and coffee routine. Needless to say, sales of Krispy-Kreme donuts went through the roof due in part due to Burl's knowledge of human nature.

Burl has given me kind permission to include the transcripts from the 1964 Halloween broadcast of his personal interview with Jim Williams. The transcripts are as follows. **Burl:** "Jim, when did these ghost stories originate?" **Jim:** "They started with the workmen, we had all sorts of occurrences, appearances and noises." **Burl:** " Would you give us an example?" **Jim:** " One night the brick masons were working into the late hours, very much behind schedule on the major restoration, since it was such a major under taking to do everything correctly. They were working in the basement of the house on the floors and the floors were going down as per schedule. They were finishing up when suddenly they heard lots of people upstairs running up and down the staircase." **Burl:** "And there was no one here?" **Jim:** "Well, no and there were no steps upstairs at that time; the house didn't have the foundations completed. I moved this house on this lot, you see, from the other part of town. The only way anyone could have gotten up there was to have gone past the brick masons and the basement of the house; there was a ladder going up through the staircase, through the floor. Out of curiosity, they sent one of the workmen up. Well, there was no one there. Well this wasn't too bad, except on the next night it occurred again and again and again. So one of the workmen came across the street to my apartment. He said, "Mr. Williams, there's some people over there that aren't working for you and we are all leaving!" And then I became concerned. It has a …. well it had a reaction then that meant that I was going to have a work stoppage if something didn't happen." **Burl:** " Well, did you actually discover anyone up there?" **Jim:** " No, and as time went on in the daytime and at night we had great numbers of noises there. I still say unidentified noises, being a bachelor, living in this four-story house alone, I am not superstitiously inclined, although I say we cannot identify these noises, but between twenty and thirty people have heard things here, abnormal sounds not the creaking and cracking of an old wooden house settling, you see. But it's the sort of noise that would be made by people breaking furniture up, knocking doors down, walking heavily or laughing and talking in low mumbled voices." **Burl:** "Well, has anyone actually seen anyone up there?" **Jim:** " (laughs) I'm afraid they have; we have an old gray-haired gentleman in a dressing gown that appears regularly with a white cravat and you never know where he is going to show up next. He was reported as recently as two days ago in the upstairs window glaring down on St. Julian Street. **Burl:** " Really? Were you home at the time?" **Jim:** " No, no. That's when we had some local publicity about the house and I had decided that since probably a lot of people would be by visiting that I would evade the whole thing and leave so I went shark fishing that day on my island. The house was completely empty and securely locked. Late that afternoon, a lady in the real estate business here in town told me that she had seen someone in the house and, before she knew how old I was—-I'm not old and gray-haired yet—-ah, that she thought that it was me standing in the window and six or eight people saw this man and he was standing there in sort of a mourning robe with a white cravat. He was gray-haired and was looking down his nose at the people in the street. There were all manner of people there out of curiosity observing the house and suddenly he turned his back and she said, now that I remember, he did-n't walk away; he simply vanished! **Burl:** "Just like a ghost!" **Jim:** "Yes, I suppose so." (laughs) **Burl:** "Jim, getting back to this business of your workmen and their reluctance to continue working. Did this actually slow down the schedule of renovation on the house?" **Jim:** "Well, tremendous-ly so. I was very much shaken up by it. In fact, I was so much shaken up by it that at the end of last year (1963), I discussed this entire thing with friends of mine and they said that they had once lived in a house that had strange—they just simply said, once lived in a haunted house—they didn't say strange in the way I referred to them and they had had the house exor-cised and suggested that I have it exorcised." **Burl:** "Now, will you explain just what that is?" **Jim:** "Well, the rites of exorcism is the rite itself as recorded in the Church of England's prayer book. Very few American prayer books have this Rite of Exorcism listed now, but it is still a part of the American churches rite as well. I had the Bishop, Bishop Stewart of the State of Georgia, The Episcopal Bishop of the State of Georgia, exorcise this house which is very unusual. He performed the ceremony standing in the eighteenth-century drawing room upstairs here in front of all the work-men and in front of several friends of mine. **Burl:** "What is this? Is this a kind of dedication on the house, or what?" **Jim:** "It's more or less of a blessing ceremony, but it is also an exorcism rite. In other words it com-mands the evil spirit and forces it to leave the premises and for, as he put it the arch angels of the Lord to dwell herein. It is very interesting."

Burl: "Any other unusual instances?" **Jim:** "Well, there was one real good one. Unfortunately, it happened one night when I was not here. Three of my friends were outside—this is in the early history of the house, I mean, early history associated with me. The brick masons again threw their tools down and headed for St Julian Street and said they weren't going to work anymore. My three friends, one of them is a research scientist, a very much non-believer—again, I mention that for a purpose—in the supernatural, the other one is an advertising artist, and the third one is a very athletic young man, a life guard, and again, i.e. he's not afraid of anything. They were standing outside and the brick masons fled out from St. Julian Street all upset and they asked them "what's going on?" and they said the house is filled with those same so and so noises and so the little guy, the life guard, said "Well, I'll find out what's going on!" The other two, my two friends, along with the brick mason, stayed outside. He went all through the house. It was tremendously late in the afternoon, and it was just getting dark. He went all through the house and when he got up to my bedroom floor which is next to the top floor, he raised the window and he said "There's nobody up here, how ridiculous!" So the brick masons got into their cars, and they left, and my two friends went into their apartment directly across from my restored house here and all of a sudden they heard a scream and they came out. They did not see anything, and when they went through the house, they could not find the young man. They finally found him on the top floor; he was stretched out next to an open chimney shaft that went four stories down to a concrete slab in the basement. They took him across the street to the apartment and tried to sort of bring him around and they said, "What happened?" and he said," Well, on three stories of the house I found nothing and on the fourth story just out of curiosity drawn up to the fourth story, and when I got to the center of the room he said it was as if I walked into a pool of cool water and I lost all control over my bodily movement. I was being drawn towards this open chimney shaft as though by a force and he said when he was a few feet away he felt that the only way he could control the situation was to just try to fall on the floor for which he did successfully, fortunately, on his back only a foot and a half from the shaft. He would have been killed surely, but this gets better. He was seated there with the two of those people in sort of a triangular form in the living room and one of my friends said, "Well, the only thing I know that Jim Williams could do is have the house exorcised. At the exact moment that he said 'exorcised' a woman's voice, a scream came from the center, the center space between the three of them, the open space. Well, the scientist, Mr. Doubting Thomas himself, shot up in the air and said, "What on earth was that?" and at that moment just seconds from the first scream there was a second scream again between the three of them. The young man went into sort of a semi-trance—-he was so shook up about the whole thing. This was the worst occurrence we have had. They heard a noise outside; they went to the door, and they looked across at the house and they saw what they thought was a figure, well of me; they thought they saw me standing at the top window. This was the first known appearance of the man in the white jacket with the cravat, the white, silk cravat. That was rather startling; I was out at a dinner party that night and

44

when I came back they had decided not to tell me about it because I was to move into the house in less than a week's time. I finally extracted the story from them and felt very uneasy about the situation and not being able to explain it. I think most things have explanations but since I have been here in this house sometimes I wonder." **Burl:** "Thank you very much, Jim Williams, and good luck to you as I do have another appointment and I guess I better be moving along It isn't that I believe in ghosts, but the hour is getting a little late. Thank you again. This is Burl Womack, reporting for Monitor."

There was added an interesting footnote to the story. Not long after Jim Williams gave Burl the Halloween interview, he broke his leg in two places while inspecting the house on the second floor drawing room. It was late evening and dark when he stepped on a pile of two by fours. Just a short time after Jim moved in, he felt an eerie presence manifesting itself throughout the house. He was awakened by the sound of something walking around and around his bed. Upstairs came loud banging and crashing sounds and when he pursued the instigator of the calamity, he witnessed doors closing and locking themselves, but he never spotted the culprit.

Jim Williams had many more tales to tell about his time living in the Hampton Lillibridge house. One time he found a maid waiting for him outside underneath the carport when he returned home from an important antique auction. She was thoroughly frightened and disconcerted by what she said was a powerful masculine presence in the house. She fled the house immediately and waited for Mr. Jim when she heard the grinding of chains in the living room. Far too afraid to re-enter the house, she waited for his return and later left his employ as had several others for the same reason. There had been an empty burial crypt discovered by workmen under Jim's house but workers told him it was empty. The crypt was made of materials used during colonial times called tabby. Tabby was comprised of a hard concrete substance made from the combination of lime and oyster shells. It is no wonder that no body was ever found in the crypt. After 200 years, few colonial corpses have survived. Most have returned to the soil from which they came. Ashes to ashes and dust to dust, as it says in the Bible. Neighbors and even those who just passed by the Hampton Lillibridge house have reported sightings of phantoms in the windows, parties, and music playing when no one is at home through the years. The current owners are very happy with their famous haunted house. A plaque still remains outside the home stating "Private Residence." Tour guides are leading tours by the house every day, which I feel makes the spirits who live there feel very welcome in Savannah.

Outside Harley Davidson Shop on East River Street

Photo by Kathleen Thomas

Photo by Sandra Mudge

Hamilton-Turner House

Chapter Eight

Known Haunted Sites You Must
Visit In Savannah, Georgia

If you really want an exciting and ghost-filled time while you are in Savannah, stay at a hotel or bed and breakfast in the historical downtown area. Just walking the old cobblestones along River Street, its cotton warehouses now converted into antique shops, candy stores, and a host of other delightful restaurants and shops, you will find yourself and friends and family in the midst of early Georgia history. The old warehouses have their own stories to tell, and modern day proprietors have experienced ghosts and haunting specters even today. In the past few years two different shops located in the rear of Trustees Garden next to the Pirates House Restaurant on East Broad street experienced ghosts firsthand. They both have since moved away from the building where these incidents occurred. The shop located downstairs opened as normal with the owner and her sales clerk preparing for another long day of retailing. The door opened and in walked the first customer of the day. In retailing, the most important customer to sell an item to is the first face you see. Psychologically, making this sale will help you focus on successfully closing sales the rest of the day. The young clerk approached the elderly lady with a smile and a welcome "good morning, may I help you?" The little woman said nothing but continued walking past the clerk as if she weren't there. The store owner looked up and witnessed the attempt her clerk had made towards the lady customer and felt the woman was being quite rude by not answering her. The little woman continued to walk past the two of them and disappeared through a solid brick wall at the rear of the store. They both looked at each other in disbelief knowing they had witnessed a ghost.

The owner directly upstairs from the previous gift shop was opening her shop one morning and had the distinct feeling she was being watched. Out of the corner of her eye she spied a little boy hiding in a dark corner of her shop. She unlocked the door, turned on the lights and approached the spot where she had last seen him but he was gone. For some time she had noticed that certain articles including stuffed animals, child's furniture and

47

toys had been moved around the store from where she displayed them. The next day as she returned to the shop she had the same eerie feeling of eyes watching her. She unlocked the door and immediately noticed that a rocking horse and many other toys had been moved and played with in the center of the store overnight. The phantom child continued for a while to visit her store but eventually moved on. Perhaps he grew lonely by not having another child spirit there to play with. We may never know the answer to this bizarre haunting.

You can feel a thick veil of timelessness that sets the downtown area apart, as opposed to the more fast-paced, modern nature of south side Savannah. There is an overall feeling of stepping back in time when you walk the streets of historical Savannah, as if you have been propelled one hundred years into the past.

The shade of the moss-covered oaks and elms in the beautiful parks, the architectural delights, the congeniality of Savannah's townspeople, all beckon, and the Savannah Historic Foundation, founded in 1955, has done an outstanding job in revitalizing the area and helping homeowners comply to rules and regulations regarding signs , colors, etc. to maintain historic authenticity.

Plan to spend a good amount of time in the north end of Savannah as well since the earliest buildings, battlefields, cemeteries, churches, forts, funeral homes, hospitals, homes, hotels, old jails, orphanages, restaurants, schools, stadiums, theatres and warehouses are filled with imprints of living history from today and the past. Begin your journey from River Street inland.

There are multitudes of haunted sites along River Street. The following list provides a few sites of both historical and paranormal interest:
- The Shrimp Factory Restaurant at 313 East River Street
- The Harley Davidson shop at 503 East River Street,
- The old Cotton Exchange building and the surrounding warehouses
- Jere's Antiques at 9 North Jefferson
- The Pirates House at 20 East Broad Street
- The Marshall House Hotel at 123 East Broughton Street
- The Pink House Restaurant at 23 Abercorn Street
- The Colonial Cemetery at Abercorn and Oglethorpe
- The Davenport House at 324 East State
- The KeHoe House at 123 East Habersham
- 1790 Inn and Restaurant at 307 East President Street
- Owens Thomas House at 124 Abercorn Street
- The Hampton Lillibridge House at 507 East St. Julian Street
- The Green-Meldrim House next to Saint John's Cathedral at 1 West Macon Street
- The Juliette Gordon Lowe House at 10 East Oglethorpe Avenue
- The Andrew Lowe House at 329 Abercorn Street

- The Scarbrough House on West Broad Street
- The Hamilton-Turner Inn at 330 Abercorn Street
- Laurel Grove Cemetery
- The old Chandler Hospital, built in 1819, on Abercorn Street
- The Telfair Hospital on Drayton and East Park Ave.

This list is just a small sampling of truly haunted areas that have had both past and present spirits haunting them.

In addition, many of the areas old forts are of interest as well. Don't forget to visit old Fort Wayne, next to the Pirate's House and Trustee's Garden. It was built in 1759 and was originally called Fort Savannah. Other forts to see are Fort Jackson, Fort Pulaski, and Fort Mcallister in Richmond Hill, Georgia. After you wade through these sites, a must see is Bonaventure Cemetery and The Bethesda Home for Boys. The pure history you will learn from each site is compelling all on its own. Once you factor in all the ghost tales, you will understand why Savannah deserves her reputation as "the most haunted city in America!"

Paranormal activity has also been reported in many downtown homes. Homes on Price and President, as well as at an 1810 old wood frame townhouse in the 300 block of West Charlton, on the corner of State and Lincoln, and on West Gordon and Liberty Streets. The cottages at 426 East Saint Julian Street, East Taylor, East Jones, and East Gordon are being touted as haunted by citizens living in these neighborhoods. There have also been many reports of items moving around apartments and townhouses on their own. Phantom spirit sightings are almost a daily occurrence. A friend of mine actually saw a full-figured woman floating through one wall and out the next of his office downtown! The reports of people feeling and seeing these apparitions has been growing year by year. I feel more and more people are open minded and can therefore see these entities that they couldn't see before. Sightings do happen but not to everybody. It takes a combination of an open mind, the proper atmosphere, and the urging of a spirit wanting to communicate with you to make it happen. For some people, it is a once in a lifetime thing, for others a daily occurrence.

Photo by Sandy Mudge

Photo by Sandy Mudge

Chapter Nine

Why is it Called Tourist Season if We Can't Shoot at Them?
...George Carlin

Springtime in Savannah, Georgia is filled with the most colorful array of flora and fauna in all of God's green earth! This time of year is very spiritual as well as beautiful. The camellias blossom in profusion in manicured backyard gardens lineup like debutants at a ball. Although a native of Asia, the camellia took root well in southern soil and has proliferated here for centuries. The variously colored trees and shrubs were named for Georg Josef Kamel (1661-1706), who studied botany.

One can't miss the millions of azalea shrubs with their brilliant evergreen leaves and pink, white, and rose petals growing almost everywhere you look around historic houses and grand parks all over Savannah. The hundreds of thousands who visit Savannah every year come to the St. Patrick's Day Parade and celebration. The largest get-together of its kind in the South, between 300,000 to 500,000 tourists gather on March 17th. The fountain in Forsyth Park flows shamrock green and everyone is an Irishman for a day. It is a very joyful occasion for friends and relatives alike.

Whether it's bright and sunny or even if a light drizzle or rain should come on the celebration date (which happens on occasion), there is a feeling of time standing still and there is an aura of déjà vu. The feeling is a timeless one and as the end of the celebration nears you are quietly transplanted to the here and now to enjoy another day visiting Savannah, Georgia.

Savannah's cemeteries are truly a spiritual place to visit and are filled with history and wonderful works of art in the tombstones and statues memorializing our forefathers. There is no death. Life is abundant and everlasting. We witness friends and family lovingly tending to the graves and tombs of those who have passed over. They see us from the other side and are attracted to those they love and or sympathize with and will often try for the good of the recipient to leave a mental message or imprint to influence or warn of danger.

I have visited many cemeteries in the past and I always have a strong feeling of peaceful souls at rest and yet upon occasion an invitation to return for a visit. There is a strong connection that leads me to the conclusion that we are all one in the spirit, both the living and the dead. In 1 John Chapter 3, verse 2, the apostle writes:

Beloved, now we are the sons of God, and it doth not yet appear what we shall be: but we know that, when he shall appear, we shall be like him: for we shall see him as he is.

I have been asked by many tourists about the possibility of taking home (unintentionally of course) a spirit with them when visiting a cemetery on a ghost tour or otherwise. There have indeed been cases where people have been followed home by spirits after visiting a cemetery as documented in earlier chapters of this book. But, as president Franklin Delano Roosevelt once said, "We have nothing to fear but fear itself!" My suggestion to them is to say the Lord's Prayer, Matthew: Chapter 6, verses 9-13,

After this manner therefore pray ye: Our Father which art in heaven, Hallowed be thy name. Thy kingdom come. Thy will be done in earth, as it is in heaven. Give us this day our daily bread. And forgive us our debts, as we forgive our debtors. And lead us not into temptation, but deliver us from evil: for thine is the kingdom, and the power, and the glory, for ever. Amen. Ask the lord to shield you, and those with you, in a white light and you are good to go .

Kathy Thomas demonstrates the use of a laser digital thermal scanner.

Chapter Ten

The Importance of High Technology in Ghost Investigations

Beside the normal senses of seeing, hearing, touching, smelling, and feeling, ghost investigations have gotten more precise with the advent of technology over the last twenty-five years. We now know how to record energy anomalies at haunted sites through infrared monitors using high speed photographic film. Science is now on the side of the ghost hunters who strive to prove to all the skeptics in the world who do not believe in survival after death. Modern equipment can now document survival phenomena. It is no longer necessary simply to take eyewitness accounts of haunted sites as the only evidence of spirit activity.

My paranormal study group, *The Searchers*, were called in to investigate several unusual sightings and strange happenings in a home of a mother and daughter on the southside of Savannah, Georgia. The reported sightings of not one but three spirits that had manifested themselves in the kitchen, the bedroom, and outside in the backyard. Not all manifestations are necessarily ghosts. Energy implants left over from the previous homes owners can have either a positive or negative effect on what the current inhabitants may be feeling or experiencing. The young lady and her mother had both seen a kind and gentle spirit of a petite thirty-year-old woman standing by the sink in the kitchen. She turned and smiled at them and then slowly faded away. The mother thought she recognized the entity as her mom at the age of thirty. Previous owners of the house told the mother and daughter that they had experienced sightings of an old man standing in the bedroom. They had lived there for twenty-five years and seen him often. This was the second phantom seen in the house and he was always in a bad mood when he was seen standing at the foot of the daughter's bed. The dark energy of this ghost frightened the young woman so much that she couldn't rest and nightmares seemed to close in around her. One night she dreamed the old man had picked her up and was mumbling some bizarre language she could not understand. Another dream had him throwing her up against the bedroom wall. Both dreams were so real to her that they disturbed her greatly.

The daughter had taken a roll of film filled with various shots of her bedroom at Christmas but when developed the pictures came out black except for one photo that had a figure of a man standing in the middle of white smoke.

Our group arrived about dusk, unloaded our equipment, and walked up to the front door. The daughter greeted us and we were soon interviewing her and her mom who was busy in the kitchen icing a chocolate layer cake that used Coca Cola in the recipe. A number of our group spanned out into the home and through the garage and back yard. I was among the first to go back to the extreme rear of the backyard at the fence and soon began to feel a funny sensation on the ground around my feet. It was if my pants leg was being pulled on and a cool breeze ran up the leg of my pants. I took a number of photographs to the left and right of the area where I stood. Then I returned to the house and inquired of the mother if she had ever buried any pets in the area that I had the strange psychic sensation in and she said, "Yes, we have buried all the family pets there for many years!" The family that had lived there before us had also buried many beloved pets there but no permanent markers were used. They had tied small crosses with string and pushed them into the ground. The little grave sites would soon fall into disrepair with wind and weather and disappear.

I could feel a mild chill on my face and hands as I recounted the experience in the back yard. I had taken many pictures that evening but only the back yard photos showed small rounded luminosities that were bright and hovering over the site of the unmarked pet cemetery in the rear of the yard. We call these luminosities *orbs*. They cannot be seen with the naked eye but do turn up on film and are one of the best evidences one can ascribe to a genuine haunting. Other members in our group also got these *orbs* in their shots. We used five different kinds of cameras and film. Orbs appear to be energy from an unknown origin. All the orbs we captured on film did not show up in front of our eyes nor could they be detected on an infrared motion detector. All of our shots were from different angles and the orbs seemed to change directions and defy gravity. They were seen partially on the ground as well as high in the trees overhanging the backyard. The orbs seemed to multiply before us and seemed to react to our presence.

Meanwhile in the daughter's back bedroom our members all had the distinct impression of a malevolent spirit pervading the atmosphere in the room. My son Lee Cobb got a headache that was so overwhelming that he had to go out of the house to my car to recuperate. Everyone agreed that that room made us very uncomfortable and we all felt a intense pressure that seemed to make us feel ill. I had a headache that went on for several hours after Lee and I had returned home from the investigation.

One of our members said he could see the image of an old man standing upright menacingly at the foot of the bed and glaring at him, and then simply vanishing. We completed our investigation that night and were contacted by the daughter the following day that the room felt better and she was able to sleep there peacefully again. The e-mail she sent thanked our group and told us she felt the room was lighter and her fears about sleeping there had subsided.

The third spirit seen outside the house along the fence may be the ghost of a fifteen-year-old boy. He was killed in a tragic accident next door when he rode his bicycle through the yard. The young man wasn't paying close attention and had his head turned in the opposite direction when he rode full speed into a clothes line and broke his neck. The boy's spirit sometimes manifests itself along the edge of the yard and watches as mom hangs out clothes to dry. The fact was we were never really able to prove or to disprove ghosts, but we all felt a certain paranormal activity at this location.

As for other technological advances, the video camera is one of the most useful. Today the quality of the video camera has improved greatly over the old dinosaurs you had to carry on your shoulder ten years ago. The best video cameras can film in 0 Lux = (total darkness). The tiny hand- held cameras today cost less and achieve a whole lot more than their ancestors. The improvements in ghost hunting equipment include a Tri-field EMF Detector for locating electromagnetic fields and the IR Thermal Probe for measuring the temperature in on-site investigations. There are dozens of night- vision-related equipment out on the market that make seeing in the dark a little easier, but don't be fooled into believing you are seeing ghosts just because you are wearing night-vision goggles. The human eye sees up to 720 nm and scopes that are under the 980nm do very little more than illuminate the area of sight slightly.

The Remote IR Thermo-Probemeter is an awesome pocket-sized scanner that measures temperatures down to 0 degrees with pinpoint accuracy. The back-lighted display gives an instant read out by simply pressing the trigger.

Another incredible advance is in the field of *electronic voice phenomena.* The actual voices and sounds of the dead trying to communicate with the living have been captured recently by paranormal investigators all over the world. The *(EVP)* itself was discovered as early as the late nineteenth-century when Thomas Edison invented the first recording device. It became a pet project of the genius inventor to try to communicate with the dead through his invention. The quality of recording tapes has advanced greatly in the last five years and you must remember to use only fresh tapes in your recording efforts. There has been a lot of controversy over whether you are listening to a genuine spirit trying to communicate or the ghost researcher's accidental taping of his or her own movements and sounds or voices. Try this simple experiment in your home at your convenience. Leave your tape recorder on when you leave your home to go shopping. Make sure everyone is away from the house and no pets are present and turn off all air or heat. Dollars to donuts when you return and play the recorder back, you will hear a number of eerie creaks and unexplainable sounds you normally miss in the course of our everyday hectic modern lives.

I tried this at my house and got footsteps, the sound of cabinets opening and closing and even a cough! I stress that the whole family was out at the time I made the recording. EVP is still being researched as I write this and some phenomenal voice messages have come through for those paranormal investigators willing to suffer the hours it takes to listen to tapes for messages from the other side.

Private ghost hunting organizations and paranormal investigators are using many new products to document each case of paranormal activity every day. In the not too distant future we may see even more advances in equipment for documenting evidence of the supernatural world that surrounds us.

Fort Pulaski on Cockspur Island
Photos by Sandy Mudge

Photos by Sandy Mudge

Chapter Eleven

Fort Pulaski in Savannah is a Hauntingly-Historical Fortress

Near the mouth of the Savannah River as you drive eastward toward Tybee Island is a small island called Cockspur Island. Strategically located to guard the channel stands the shell-battered walls of Fort Pulaski. The site that Fort Pulaski was built on has a long history of misery and death. King George of England recognized the location of a fortress there as key in guarding the young colony of Savannah, Georgia, from the Spanish fleets who might decide to bombard the city from the sea. The first fort was built in 1761 and named for the King.

After the revolution the fort was named Fort Greene in 1794 for the American hero Nathaniel Greene. Only ten years after, in 1804, a great hurricane struck Tybee and washed away Fort Greene, and many of the American colonial troops stationed there were drowned.

The site was rebuilt with massive stone walls thicker than any fortress ever built prior to that time. It was considered impregnable by the standards of the late 1820's and was re-named Fort Pulaski. America owed a debt of gratitude to the Polish Army commander Count Casimir Pulaski, who aided the colonial forces during the siege of Savannah in 1779, and thus named the fort for him.

A number of volunteers captured Fort Pulaski from the the small contingent left guarding her in early 1861 just a few short months before the firing on Fort Sumter and the outbreak of The Civil War. There were no casualties in the surrender of the fort in 1861, but within the following year Union forces that were stationed at Tybee Island bombarded the walls of the fort with shells that blasted the old masonry to rubble. Eighteen years it had taken to build the fortress, but the new rifled cannon shells drilled their way into the crumbling masonry making it look like Swiss cheese.

Colonel Charles H. Olmstead surrendered the fort in April 1862. Soon after, on Thanksgiving day 1862, a ball was held in Fort Pulaski for the officers and their wives to celebrate the retaking of the fort. Colonel Olmstead's sword that he surrendered was carried off as war booty and stayed in the same family till it was returned to the fort by a family descendant in the late 1970's. The saddest episode which took place at Fort Pulaski was the inhumane treatment of the Confederate prisoners of war held captive there. Neither side took great care of its prisoners during the Civil War. Unionists resented the cruel treatment many of their men had suffered in prisoner of war camps such as the one at Andersonville Prison. Consequently, the soldiers from the North had little sympathy for the over 500 Confederates at Fort Pulaski. The photos I have seen of survivors and the dead remind me of those of the prisoners in the Nazi death camps in World War Two. Prisoners were regularly beaten, and many starved to death, their diet consisting mainly of scraps from their captors' garbage. Many suffered and died needlessly, of malnutrition, pneumonia, and scurvy. As prisoners in the casements, they were broiled to death in the summer and were frozen to death in the winter. Broken men, both mentally and physically, the survivors of the ordeal lived only a short time after their release at the end of the war in 1865.

This writer finds it difficult to imagine the agony and utter despondency these loyal Confederate men suffered through. The images and imprints left from the tragedy play back over and over to those sensitive to the vibrations who visit the Fort.

Recently, Bobbie Weyl, a member of our paranormal study group known as The Searcher's visited Fort Pulaski with a film crew from Fox Family's Scariest Places On Earth. The moment they arrived there Bobbie had the sensation come across her of men and supply wagons lined up inside the parade grounds. Bobbie led a small group of local college students by lantern through the old casements and on top to the parapet. It is understood from war time documents that a soldier was wounded and died on the parapet or heading down the stairs of the parapet. It was at this location that Bobbie felt the strongest feelings of despair and agony. The three students who attempted to spend the night at the fort heard distinct sounds of doors being shut and footsteps in front of and behind them. The two girls and one guy decided it was far too much for them to spend the night and left sometime after 3:00 A.M. They noted they also saw the phantom figure of a Civil War soldier walking along the parade grounds that night.

The film crew had various things happen to them as well, including their camera batteries dying out and strange sounds being heard in the casements of Fort Pulaski.

As time passed, Fort Pulaski became overgrown with weeds and marsh grasses until it was recognized as a national landmark in the 1930's and fell under the auspices of our national parks program. The main building has a superb display of artifacts from Fort Pulaski's past. Be sure to inspect Colonel Olmstead's sword among other fantastic Civil War items.

My family and I have visited Fort Pulaski (in daylight) many times. The incredible feeling you get as you walk through the massive gates into the parade ground and on top of the parapet is unique. The winds that seem to encircle you left and right seem to call out the emotions of the men who served time there both as prisoners and guards. The view of Tybee is grand and glorious on a sunny day, and I highly recommend you take family and friends there soon and enjoy the ambience. John Breen is the current supervisor there and is always happy to help in any way he can to make your visit there educational and fun. You can reach the national monument Fort Pulaski by writing to P.O.Box 30757, Savannah, Georgia 31410-0757.

Angel statue at Laurel Grove Cemetery

Chapter Twelve

"Yes, Virginia, Angels Really Do Exist!"

In all the years I have studied and learned about the supernatural, the subject of angels has fascinated me more than anything else. I have had several close friends and acquaintances tell me of mysterious strangers who have come out of nowhere in their time of need to rescue them from physical harm. They can suddenly appear before you and offer to aid you in your time of need and then disappear as quickly as they have come. There is never a doubt in the minds of those needing aid as to the good Samaritan offering them help is a fellow human being. But soon after the danger has passed, the friendly helper disappears into thin air.

Our Lord God has bestowed power, freedom, and great wisdom upon the holy angels and a great number of them are walking among us on earth, managing the assignments given to them. They are immortal and have existed since the dawn of time. The scriptures do not indicate how far back in history but it is presumed it was in the earliest times on Earth.

Angels do play an active part in guiding and protecting those mortals in whose charge they are given. There is absolutely no way to doubt the existence of angels in service to the Lord God. They guard the heaven and Earth. They are also known in the Bible as "ministering spirits" (Heb. 1:14). The Bible is filled with two hundred and ninety two references to angels in the old and the new testament. The Hebrew word for messenger is mal'akh . The Greeks used the word Angelos, which in English translates to "angel," meaning messenger.

Angels have watched over mankind throughout all history. They stood at the gates at the Garden of Eden; they appeared to Abraham; they saved Lot's family. An angel intervened, as well, at the sacrifice of Isaac, and Jacob had a vision with thousands of angels standing on a ladder to heaven. And they accompanied the Israelites through their trials in the desert.

Four of the greatest prophets in the Bible were aided by angels of the Lord. They were Daniel, Ezekiel, Isaiah, and Zechariah. Without angelic intervention many happy endings in the Bible would have ended in disaster.

There are three Triads or nine choirs of angels that were thought to exist according to the sixth century writer Pseudo-Dionysius the Areopagite. God created this Celestial Hierarchy much like a commander marshalling his forces into different ranks to attend to different missions.

God placed the first three groups of "Holy Angels" by his side in the heavenly throne room. These are the Seraphim, Cherubim, and the Thrones. The next three groups are the Dominions, Virtues, and Powers. The last three groups are the Principalities, Archangels, and Angels. The latter three are the most active in preventing calamities in our plane of existence. They can hear us and interact on our behalf when necessary.

The time and energy devoted to the subject of angels would fill volumes. We as human beings must take many things we truly believe in on faith alone. No matter what is said or done it is difficult to convince someone of the existence of beings who are invisible and difficult to place in our worldly context of thinking. This is why faith is so important.

In 1979 my sister Kathy Cobb was trying to get back home after completing a job interview in Garden City. It had been raining heavily there and the low lying grounds were under water. She had unintentionally driven through a deep puddle and splashed water upwards into the automobile engine.

She was driving along Bay Street when the engine began to sputter and lose power. She just had enough power to pull off to the nearest curb. She called everyone she knew but no one was able to help her. She became very upset and prayed for someone to come and rescue her. Within a few moments of praying a white truck pulled up in front of her. A tall, older gentleman with a white beard and wearing an immaculate all white painters outfit walked towards her and lightly tapped on her driver's side window. He asked, "Can I help you, young lady?" She wiped her tears and shook her head, "Yes." The man lifted the hood of her disabled car and sprayed a can of aerosol into the carburetor. He then gently pushed the hood back down till it locked and told her to turn the ignition on.

Kathy wondered to herself why this man appeared so clean and neat. Most painters are covered from cap to shoes with splotches of dried and smeared paint. This man looked as if he just walked out of a J.C. Penny's paint department catalog.

Kathy did as he said and the engine roared into life. She then reached over to the passenger seat for her pocketbook to offer the man some compensation for his time and trouble, but when she looked up he had mysteriously disappeared. He had no time to walk or even run away. She heard no engine start up nor was his white truck anywhere in sight. He had to be the angel she had prayed would come and help her.

There have been numerous times that my life was spared by what could only be an act of God. It's amazing that simply driving your car to work each day through the Savannah's Road Rage Jungle I haven't been killed.

It is truly a miracle that I am here today to write this story.

My life was saved by the United States Coast Guard off the Atlantic Beach near the May Port Naval Air Station in the late 1960s. My father, Bob Cobb, and his boss, Ed Epps, and I went fishing one weekend searching for gator trout. We had traveled a good distance from shore taking a small, fourteen-foot boat well out of the sight of land. It was my first time deep sea fishing. Before this, I had primarily fished off public docks, bridges, and the Jacksonville Beach Pier. I loved to wade out till the cool salt water of the Atlantic was level at my waist to surf cast and crab using a net and hand lines. Our boat began to rock back and forth and I had my first case of Sea Sickness. The early morning sun beat down on me as I tried to steady myself. I didn't have my sea legs as they call it in the Navy and my head was spinning around. Before long I started to get a little green around the gills. My stomach began to churn and I felt queasy. My dad and his boss thought my plight was very humorous, but I was not a happy camper. Ed Epps said if I would lay down flat on my stomach that I would soon feel better. Instead I spent a good portion of the fishing trip over the side of the boat. When I did feel like dropping a line into the water, the fish were biting at the bait with the ferocity of a school of Piranha. We caught them on every hook and line we cast out. But all the fun was short lived due to the skies getting darker and darker.

Weird stuff started happening to us, the longer we stayed out at sea. Unbeknownst to Ed, one of the kids in his neighborhood had sabotaged the boat by putting a sack of flour in the gas tank. We were just starting to return to land when the engine began to sputter and stop. To make matters worse, a serious ocean squall was creeping up all around the small craft and we knew we had to get back home as soon as possible.

As Ed was bending over the engine, his only set of pliers flew out of his hands and down into the briny deep of the Atlantic Ocean. When he was trying to catch the pliers, his glasses and cigarettes fell out of his pocket as well. I was feeling a little better and I had to stifle laughing out loud when I watched Ed lift up the collapsible boat roof and five pounds of white flour blew up in his face like a Swiss avalanche. I felt as if I were taking part in a Three Stooges comedy sketch. The wind blew stronger and the waves grew larger and more ominous. By this time the storm was upon us, and I said a silent prayer for God to save us. Ed had an emergency radio on board and called the Coast Guard stationed at Jacksonville Beach. They radioed and confirmed they would soon be out to rescue us. The storm began to worsen, the sky was black, and the waves were bouncing us around like a ping pong ball with its top caved in.

Ed got the engine to work again but we could only go about ten miles per hour in reverse only! In about twenty-five minutes we could see the Coast Guard cutting through the water to save us. I was never happier to see anyone in my entire life. From that day to this, I have never gone back out in a small boat beyond the sight of land. I credit the U.S. Coast Guard and the Lord for saving my life.

Angels do not have to be seen to influence our thoughts. They mentally project their thoughts to ours so we will respond and save a person in distress. Once, as a teenager, I spotted a young girl playing along the edge of a dangerous intersection as I was returning from running an errand. I had just looked up and watched the cars travel quickly by, just barely missing this little child by only a few feet. She would be killed if I did not act soon. People who were driving by could not see her in their field of vision. I realized the gravity of the situation. A booming voice suddenly entered my head, " Save the Child!" I reacted as quickly as I could and grabbed her and returned her to her home and told her mother what had nearly happened.

The mother had fallen asleep on the couch, and the young girl had walked out of the unlocked front door and was playing on the edge of the busy street. Although she was visibly embarrassed by the situation, the mother thanked me for saving her daughter's life.

A most unusual occurrence happened recently to a Savannah insurance broker as she was on a return flight from visiting her family across the country. She was sitting near the window at 20,000 feet and decided the view was too beautiful to miss. She grabbed her camera and took a shot at random at the beautiful sunlit clouds and then settled back in her seat and enjoyed the rest of her journey home.

When she arrived at her home in Savannah, the lady dropped off the pictures she had taken to have them developed at a local store. The pictures all came off rather well, but she was astonished to find the picture that was taken from the window of the plane had an unusual anomaly. There on a cloud was the image of a winged female angel standing in the center of the photograph! It was very shocking and mystifying to see.

Not all angels are the bright knights in shining armor, fighting for goodness and mercy. There are millions of fallen angels who are fighting on the dark side for their dark lord Satan. According to Revelation Chapter 12, one third of all the angels in heaven were tossed to the Earth. The Cardinal Bishop of Tusculum estimated in the 15th Century that the fallen angels numbered 133,306,668. They were cast down from heaven in a free fall that lasted nine days.

In conclusion, angels do exist today, as they did yesterday and as they will for all time. The prophet Paul tells us in the Bible to beware because even Satan has the capabilities of showing himself as an angel of light. If you should ever come in contact with an angel from the higher realm, ask him if he is truly an angel of the Lord God almighty and if he serves our Lord Jesus Christ. He will not be able to lie to you and will have to confess one way or the other as to his true allegiance.

"Mama, I just met my guardian angel"

Chapter Thirteen

"Mama, I Just Met My Guardian Angel"

L ittle four-year-old Whitney had just returned with the family to Ma's house for a Christmas reunion. It was to be a very sweet and very sad time for all concerned. One of the most important people in Whitney's life would not be here to celebrate Christmas this year.

Whitney's grandmother whom everyone called Ma had passed away only one month before, on November 22, 1992. This was to be the first Christmas without the family matriarch. Everyone would recount all the good times they had when Ma was alive and there was a feeling that Ma was still present and enjoying the stories that everyone was telling about her and all the good times they had as a family.

Whitney's father and uncles and aunts and cousins were standing outside the house talking when Whitney's mom walked into the house to sit down to rest. Ever since her mother's passing, Whitney's mom had been visited in her dreams by Ma. She was so real that she could touch and smell her. Whitney sat beside her mother on the comfortable old couch and reminisced about how much they both loved and missed Ma. Suddenly, Whitney's mom heard Ma's pots and pans clang in the kitchen but dismissed it as one of the other grand children.

Whitney turned and said, "Momma, I have to go potty." Momma replied, "You know where it is darlin'. Go on." Little Whitney had been gone for only a few moments when her momma heard the clanging of pots and pans a second time. She thought that Whitney was in the kitchen playing with Ma's pots and pans, but everyone else had remained outside. A few minutes later Whitney returned from the bathroom with a look of contentment." Honey, were you playing with Ma's pots and pans earlier? The little four-year-old looked up at her and said, " No, Momma." The next thing the child told her made goose bumps stand out on her arms: Whitney added that she had seen the ghostly figure of Ma standing in in front of the stove smiling at her and letting her know that everything is fine, and she is in a better place with the Lord. Whitney remembers to this very day the ghostly image cooking in the kitchen was her Ma. She feels Ma still watches and acts on her behalf as her guardian angel. Whitney feels safe and warm whenever Ma's presence is felt around her.

An even more bizarre post script to this story includes the tape that was made at the family reunion. When the video tape was later reviewed by everyone at the family get-together, there was a strange anomaly found. The tape clearly shows the storm door at the front of the house shutting, and you can see a distinct reflection of Ma on the door!

There are hundreds of case histories of scenes replaying over and over that have been captured in the atmosphere or on the surface of a material objects such as a building or other structure. It is much like a movie film projecting images on a screen played back to those who are sensitive to these projected images.

This is called a Residual Haunting. Past events are recorded in the fabric of time. This explains how a number of tourists in England have reported seeing the ghosts of Roman legions marching down roads used by them 1000 years ago during their occupation of Great Britain. Perhaps, in this case Whitney's grandmother had spent so many years and expended so much energy in her kitchen work that it left an indelible psychic impression of her appearing there. But, how can we explain the sounds of the clanging pots and pans when no one else was in the kitchen?

Photo by Sandy Mudge

18 West Oglethrorpe Avenue, Savannah, GA

Chapter Fourteen

Poltergeist Incident on
West Oglethorpe Avenue

A lady who rents an upstairs brick row-house apartment at West Oglethorpe Avenue in downtown Savannah Georgia recently contacted me to investigate poltergeist activity she had observed and experienced there. She had been in many times before buying, selling, and trading bibelots in my shop. She had found many pieces of antique jewelry and old glassware to add to her collection at home.

Recently she moved from a cute carriage house apartment on West Charlton Street to an older red brick row-house on West Oglethorpe Avenue. She leased the apartment with a couple who shared with her a number of unexplainable phenomena since moving in. The first time she showered, her shampoo bottle flew across the room. There was a definite chill around her when ever she was in certain areas of the apartment. She had the feeling of eyes staring right through her. None of these strange things happened to her in the old carriage house, but this upstairs apartment had a darker, more ominous feel to it. It was even rumored that someone had committed suicide there in the early 1920's or 1930's. Suicides always leave a bad karma and can cause those living in the house at a future date to perceive various psychic impressions left behind by the people who took their own lives.

The couple who shared the apartment were scared out of their wits by several unexplainable bangs and crashes. Their pets were often very nervous when the moon was full. One night two of the three were away from the apartment. One of the girls was visiting family across the country and the second was staying with friends across town because she feared staying in the haunted apartment. The male was by himself in the apartment with the dog close by him when the sounds began. The dogs ears stood up, and he rose to his feet whimpering at first, then barking at something in the room. A swishing type sound of a file cabinet opening and papers being tossed about came from a dark corner of the room opposite his sleeping quarters. The dog began barking loudly, his back arched and teeth bared, and carefully started walking towards the room where the sounds emanated from. It was 4 A.M. in the morning and the man's heart was up in his throat for fear a burglar may be ransacking the apartment. The man was about to get up and check the room when he felt a sudden coldness all around his bed. Then something dark hovered over him and seemed to smother him. Meanwhile, the dog was going berserk, gnashing his teeth and jumping up at his master's invisible attacker.

He felt a cold bony finger slide into his ear and push downward on the side of his head with great force. He had never been more frightened in his entire adult life. The cold finger continued to grind into his ear while he tried to wriggle out from under the extreme pressure placed on his skull.

He felt as if his head was about to explode. Panic began to overcome him. The acrid smell of burning dung pervaded his nostrils. He screamed out and the poltergeist released its powerful grip on him. He furtively glanced from one side of the room to the other. All he saw was shadows on the wall and the moonlight shimmering through the window glass. The apartment fell silent as a tomb. The dog had quit barking and laid back down beside him. He stood up and walked barefoot across the cold floor and looked in the room where the noises first occurred but saw nothing.

He checked the door locks and all the window latches, but found them all secure. He then felt a chill run down his back as he realized that whatever it was that attacked him in his sleep must still be in the locked apartment with him. He double checked all doors and closets, but whatever it was had left in the same way it came, quietly on little cat feet. Nothing of this earth had the power to do to him what he described happened to him that night in the upstairs apartment on West Oglethorpe Ave. The landlord wonders why this apartment's rental history is like a revolving door. The answer is simple. Tenants can't stay in a haunted apartment for very long with experiences like these taking place.

There have been several other attacks on sleeping individuals reported in the same two-mile radius of the historical district. One report involved a female spirit (Succubus) that latched onto the throat of a male teenager sleeping in a downstairs apartment on East Jones Street. The mother of the young man had to help pull this malevolent spirit off her struggling son by screaming at it to go away in the name of Jesus Christ. It loosened its hold on her son and left as quickly as it came. A female demon like this one is known as a Succubus. It is one of the night creatures known for thousands of years to follow Satan and his fallen angels in folklore and mythology. They attempt to copulate with human males as they are sleeping. Christian authorities in the Middle Ages stipulated that sex with demons was considered witchcraft. Children born of these unholy unions are often demons and become molesters themselves. The demon offspring are usually monstrous and hunted down and destroyed before they can cause more damage to humanity.

A demon in the form of a man who attacks a woman in her sleep is known as an Incubus. These male demons have no regenerative powers and are said to collect semen from men who have had sexually explicit dreams and have ejaculated in their sleep. The demons then take the semen and use it to impregnate women in their sleep.

Another individual, this time a woman, was sexually molested in her sleep by an Incubus on the same block of East Jones. Sexual molestation has been recorded in exorcism rites from the year 1614. Even in our day and age there have been several cases of demonic molestation that have taken place and are well documented as genuine.

Photo by Kathleen Thomas

Chapter Fifteen

The Haunted Orphanage
on Houston Street

The need for an orphanage became a priority for the English colonists in Savannah, Georgia, due to the Yellow Fever epidemic and several disastrous fires that claimed the lives of hundreds of people.

Life in the Georgia colony was extremely difficult, and the life span of a eighteenth-century Georgian was half of what it is today. In the 1820's, the first orphanage for females was founded on 117 Houston at the corner.

The first owner was a flamboyant First Baptist minister named Henry Cunningham. The two story orphanage is on the North West corner of Houston Street adjacent to Greene Square. The orphanage was the home of two little girls who were trapped upstairs and died in a fire. It was not recorded who these little girls were, but previous owners of the house have seen them. The little girls play an active role in many strange and bizarre sightings and are behind the supernatural activity taking place there.

The two ghost children were known to be inseparable in life and are bonded as sisters in death. They have materialized in front of many eye witnesses who have been guests of previous owners. One evening the girls were seen standing at the foot of the bed in front of an astonished friend who was staying over that weekend.

The orphanage was split down the middle and converted into a residential property a good number of years ago. Residents staying on both sides have heard children playing and chasing after one another on the stairways. In the extreme heat of the summer, cold chills can be felt in the kitchen and at the foot of the staircases. Lights come on and go off by themselves, and no matter which television station is on when viewers leave the room, the channel will be switched to cartoons when they return from their break.

The little girls love to play pranks on residents, such as hiding the cell phone and going through the ladies lingerie drawer. There was even a report of a Savannah policeman who was called out to see the two little girls who were observed playing outside in Greene Square in the daytime by a concerned citizen who thought their mom was being irresponsible.

The girls may well have died in the attic upstairs over the room of one previous owner who says there are still boards in the attic that are singed from the fire directly over her bedroom. She complains that since moving into the house her sleep patterns have changed drastically. She wakes up and can't get back to sleep from 1 – 3AM every night. She said everything in her life has changed, and she has never been so physically tired and drained of energy.

Local psychic and member of the Searchers, a paranormal study group, Bobbie Weyl investigated the site and could hear the little girls laughing and giggling at all of us trying to zero in on their whereabouts. It was all a game of hide and seek to them and their laughing caused Bobbie to laugh and giggle so hard she had to put her hand over her mouth. The little girl spirits were attracted to Bobbie because she reminded them of the grandmother figure who presided over the orphanage at the time they were alive. Their "grandma" was short and happy and pleasantly plump. She made the girls laugh. After they died, they missed seeing their adopted "grandma." Our on-site investigation fascinated the little girls, who were intrigued that so much care and attention was being spent on a search for them. Bobbie said they were standing right in front of us the entire time. We just could not see them or communicate with them on their level. They did not materialize for us but wondered why we could not see them. Bobbie was the only one who they trusted to make their presence known to during one of two investigations there.

According to eyewitnesses, the girls can pop up suddenly wearing a thin, period nightgown and shawl over their shoulders. While the girls do not play mean tricks on their hosts, the cats stay downstairs and rarely go upstairs near the ghostly duo. Hand prints of little girls hands have been seen on the attic window pane, and even after the panes have been cleaned, the children's prints have reappeared.

One young boy saw the girls at 3:00 P.M. in broad daylight. He confided to his mom the girls have long blonde hair and both were seen wearing the same nightgowns and shawls that other eyewitnesses have verified. The hair dryer and other household appliances turned on without human intervention. Other inanimate objects such as a candle and a spoon moved in front of witnesses. The pictures on the wall were turned at different angles. From everything discovered from the investigation of the orphanage and the evidence gathered from eyewitness accounts there, it is very difficult to determine what type of haunting is going on there. It may be a combination of many things, and whether you are a skeptic or an ardent believer in the supernatural, this much I do know: there is far more paranormal activity at this location than you can experience anywhere else in Savannah, Georgia.

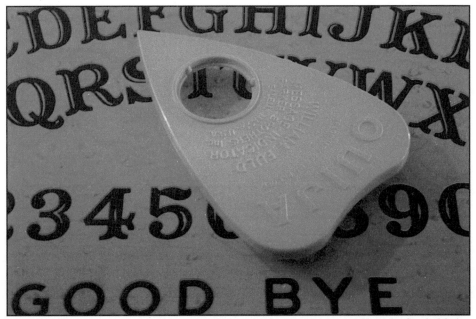

Photo by Sandy Mudge

Chapter Sixteen

The Possible Dangers of
Using The Ouija Board

I used to drag out my Ouija Board out of the closet and play with it like any other board game. It was just another piece of cardboard with numbers and letters spread out and the words yes and no on opposite ends. I never really looked at it as a way of communicating with the dead or disincarnated spirits'partially because it was sold in bookstores and toy stores as a game.

But truth is always stranger than fiction, as the history of the Ouiji Board will attest. The origin of the name Ouija is a topic of debate between many who believe that it is a combination of the French oui for yes and the German Ja for yes. The other speculation for the Ouija name is from a furniture and coffin maker from Maryland named E.C. Reiche, who made the earliest version of the board to communicate with the dead. He claimed that the name Ouija was Egyptian for luck, and a spirit had told him through a session with the board to name it so. Ouija is not Egyptian for luck, but he kept the name anyway.

Charles Kennard was a friend of E.C. Reiche and saw the potential the Ouija Board could have if mass produced. He purchased the rights to the product and founded the Kennard Novelty Company. The first mass-produced boards came out and were a hit with spiritualists and the curious alike. The shop foreman of the Kennard Novelty Company left their employ and produced Ouija Boards under the name of Fuld's Talking Boards. He quit his job and revised and promoted the game full time. William Fuld became a wealthy businessman but success did not save him from jumping to his death from a tall office building in downtown Baltimore, Maryland, in 1927.

In 1966 Parker Brothers purchased the rights to the game from Fuld's heirs. They market it as a game for entertainment purposes. The Ouija Board's reputation among religious groups is definitely negative. They say to stay away from it as you would the plague. In their opinion it is not for good for anything but evil and may entangle the user in demonic possession. As eerie as this sounds, there have been reports of teen suicides and mental breakdowns attributed to the use of the Ouija Board reported in magazines and newspapers. A lot of these negative images about Ouija Boards are the product of Hollywood's slant on making the boards objects of pure evil and presenting them to the public as such in films. It could possibly be dangerous to use if you do not fully understand that a "talking board" may actually open up a doorway to an entity that could be either good or evil. If you have no experience in this area, I suggest you speak with an informed individual who has had experience with the board. If you contact a spirit, ask it if it is a servant of the Lord God and Jesus Christ. If it is still or hesitates in its reply, break communication immediately and put the board away.

When a group of like-minded individuals use a Ouija Board, it is the subconscious mind of either one or all of them that can actually cause the planchette to move and spell out messages. The players may not know they have the ability to provide the information that comes to light during the session. ESP impressions are processed in our subconscious mind. It is this telepathic contact with the linked minds of those playing that influences the movement of the Ouija Board marker, answering their personal questions and concerns.

Family and friends I am close to have all had bizarre things happen to them when they have used a Ouija Board. The planchette flew off the table in one case when contact had been made. They have sworn to me that contact had been achieved with various spirits who claimed to have been killed in a car wreck or other calamity. There is no way to know for sure who is right or wrong on the question of whether the Ouija Board is safe to use or not.

The Frenchman M. Planchette invented the heart shaped pointer we call the planchette used with the Ouija board. The first planchettes made had two wheels on the base and a pencil. The pencil was placed with the point face down to record the writing of spirits on paper. The modern planchette has three stubby legs and a magnifier to point out words and messages from the other side.

A number of the world's gifted mediums and psychics credit the Ouija Board as their benefactor for helping them discover their psychic abilities.

The Spiritualist movement in the 1850's spurred on many of the living to try to communicate with the dead. The use of the board grew by leaps and bounds during times of war. This was a time people tried their hardest to reach their deceased loved ones. The Civil War, The Spanish-American War of 1898, World War One, World War Two, Korea and Viet-Nam are examples of the times when the Ouija Board sold in the largest numbers.

After studying this situation closely, I wholeheartedly advise against the use of Ouija Boards at any time. They can be dangerous if in the wrong hands and even more dangerous if used by one person. They aren't proof of nor can you acknowledge the existence of the spirit world using them.

Photo by Al Cobb

Chapter Seventeen

The West York Street Poltergeist

One of the most frightening episodes of poltergeist activity took place from 1996 to 1999 at 305 West York Street. The four-story townhouse is within 1/2 block of the Chatham County Courthouse. Hundreds of people pass by every day not suspecting the Circa 1822 structure houses one of the most powerful poltergeists to ever make itself known in Savannah, Georgia.

The couple who purchased the house in 1996 had big plans to restore the house to its previous grandeur. The house had a history dating back to 1820 when work began on the foundation. Within two years, work was completed. It was a splendid house with heart-of-pine floors and custom bricked fire places with high ceilings and beautiful crown moldings.

The house was owned in the 1880's by the Tuten family and it remained in the family till 1996. In the 1920s the four-story house had been converted to apartments. There was a downstairs apartment in the front and a garden apartment in the inner courtyard. There were multiple rooms rented inside the main structure as well. There was serious damage done by some of the tenants who opened gas lines and lit fires, which consequently raged out of control and burned inside the house and the upstairs attic.

There was a history of bad karma that the new owners had no idea existed until they moved into the house in 1996. They had purchased the home from a niece of the Tuten family who lived there for years.

Little quirky things started to happen when doing simple chores around the house. Phillips-head screws in the kitchen were mysteriously replaced by flat-head screws. This happened many times and got to be almost a normal thing to go wrong. Lights began to cut themselves on and off without human intervention. Two or three nights a week an unplugged radio played loudly at 3:00 A.M., but would shut itself off when the door was opened to the room it played in. Household keys were constantly being moved from where the husband and wife knew they had laid them down last. The same kind of thing happened with the television remote. The poltergeist hid it underneath or behind furniture or cabinets. Power tools were found moved around or missing and then found later in strange places.

The wife started to feel as if a presence was around her and felt someone was beside her in bed when her husband was outside the bedroom. In 1998-99 the wife was pregnant and called on her husband to go down to the midtown Kroger for a container of ice cream. He returned in a short while and she asked him where the ice cream was? She was craving a bowl ASAP! He told her he was sorry and that he had left it downstairs on the kitchen cabinet. He looked everywhere, but the ice cream was nowhere to be found. He returned to the car parked outside and no ice cream was on the seat, nor had the container fallen to the floor.

He was totally perplexed but ran back upstairs to tell the wife he would return to the store and bring her another container of ice cream, pronto. Weeks later, while entertaining guests, the husband found the container of ice cream in the liquor cabinet behind a bottle he was pulling out for a friend. The ice cream was melted but had not spoiled from being in the cabinet all that time. He showed his wife, they had a laugh over it, and he tossed it out in the trash. He was relieved to know he wasn't going crazy. But this poltergeist was beginning to get on the nerves of both of them.

Two horrific incidents happened after the birth of their child that led the couple to sell the house and leave the historic district. It seemed to the husband that the further they got into the completion of the restoration of the house, the more the poltergeist would play its games.

One afternoon for no reason a pane of glass exploded out of its framework on the stairway landing, nearly injuring two girls and a baby in the house. There was no storm or wind blowing outside to cause the freak accident.

The coupe de gras that sent them packing happened when the wife and baby were home alone and a big wooden door rocked off its hinges and slid towards the wife, nearly missing her and the baby. It crashed against the wall from thirty feet across the room! They could have been killed or severely injured by the heavy wooden door. This was the straw that broke the camel's back, so they sold the home and moved completely across town. The poltergeist had turned malevolent and gave them no other choice.

Photo by Sandy Mudge

Chapter Eighteen

Spectres at the Juarez Restaurant

A good ghost researcher doesn't like to operate on an empty stomach Downtown Savannah has a multitude of fine eating facilities all around the historic district and centering on Broughton Street. If you enjoy good Mexican food as much as I, you will find Juarez Mexican Restaurant an excellent choice.

They are located at 402 East Broughton Street on the North West corner at Price Street and Broughton Street in an old Victorian building. Besides the best Mexican cuisine, reasonable prices, and fast service, they also have a resident ghost. It is not as widely known as are the specials on the menu, but more than a few employees, including the manager, Kris White, told the Searchers that he heard his name called out from the downstairs basement when no one was in the building. The security cameras captured dark ghostly forms crossing along the rear basement walls. Two members of the Searchers, Kathy Thomas and Sandra Mudge, who eat at the restaurant often felt a cold chill in the rear of the first floor and felt a heaviness in the air. It is not known if we experienced a true haunting or the aura of an unhappy spirit there.

Broughton Street has always been the main business area in bustling uptown Savannah, Georgia. Since late in the 17th century, the Georgia gentry carriage trade sought quality merchandise from the silver smiths, cobblers, haberdashers, beauticians, dry goods stores, naval stores, opticians, blacksmiths, jewelers, and a host of other service-oriented businesses that lined both sides of the street.

All of our predecessors' business endeavors and daily routines left an impression in the atmosphere that one can still physically sense. There is a definite feel that you are walking through a doorway to the past when you stand anywhere in the historic downtown district. It may well be the beauty of the southern mansions and spectacular flora and fauna that set the mood, but I always feel a sense of deja vu. The layout of the parks and squares add to the spiritual appeal of Savannah. The downtown experience makes you feel as if you have stepped back in a time machine to the nineteenth century. You may feel a sense that a gentle spirit has just walked through you or passed by close to you. You may simply tell yourself that it's only a breeze, when it can be a benign spirit enjoying a stroll along side you. There are physical impulses from these imprints of days long passed that replay again and again that sensitive people often pick up. Just because you may not feel the same pull is no reason to believe you lack sensitivity. Everyone of us is born with a psychic mind built into us at birth; some are more developed than others. The occupants of the Juarez Restaurant may be experiencing what I have described as a Residual Haunting.

The waiters and residents living above the Juarez Restaurant are routinely working in the same general space that hundreds of other souls spent hours toiling and living in. These very brick and mortar walls are capable of absorbing all the sights and sounds of the previous restaurants, bars, and grocery stores that existed in that location. Voices, music, glasses clinking, sights and cigarette smells are replaying over and over as if recorded in a movie studio. Man's electromagnetic nature extends far beyond our physical body. God placed the living spirit in all of us, and this spirit will leave impressions of whatever we do our whole lives. We leave mental impressions on everyone we have ever come in contact with as well, hopefully good ones. This is the heart and soul of our conscious mind that lives on forever. We do leave our foot prints in the sand and God makes sure they are never washed away. Believe in his son, Jesus Christ and your imprint on the book of life will never be erased and you will live forever in the kingdom of God. According to a Gallop poll taken years ago, one in four Americans believe in ghosts and one in ten have reported seeing an apparition at some point in their lives. No matter what race or cultural background you may be, the ghosts of all mankind are believed to exist in every corner of the earth.

In the 1950's the United States Government started Project Bluebook to investigate and study the possible existence of UFO's. I am positive that more people are eye witnesses to ghostly phenomena than have seen UFO's.

It is far more of a priority to the U. S. Government to study these reports because if we ever do encounter an advanced alien race we could benefit greatly from their technology. That is going on the assumption that they are friendly and willing to help mankind. I believe we are not alone in the universe and there can be no doubt that life exists on other worlds but that is not my area to comment any further on. I love to study Earth's history and the knowledge of those who came before us.

With all these sightings of apparitions you would think our inquisitive United States Government would have a department created to study the paranormal. They must believe that the dead have nothing to teach us but one important aspect comes to my mind, if mankind does not learn from his history he is doomed to repeat all the mistakes he has made in the past. I believe benign spirits watch over us and try to help us in doing what is right and steering us away from repeating the   tragedies of the past. I believe we all have spirit guides who lend a hand and sometimes have to push us in the right directions.

Photo by Kathleen Thomas

Chapter Nineteen

The Surrency Family Ghost

Maurice Bray was sorting through his mail when he spotted a large envelope from the Wade Hampton Hotel in Columbia, South Carolina. It was postmarked Savannah, Georgia, September 16th 1940. The return address was from his nephew F.S. Miller in Millen, Georgia.

When opened, the envelope had a clipping from the Atlanta Journal Magazine dated August 15th 1940. The clipping was the full story about "The Ghost that Threw Bricks" by Madolyn Surrency Roberts, youngest surviving family member of the Surrency family in Surrency, Georgia.

I received a copy of The Surrency Ghost story from a very dear customer, Martha Summerell, in my antiques shop. She had read about our family's poltergeist experiences and thought I would appreciate this spectacular ghost tale. How right she was! Martha's niece in Jacksonville, Florida, owns one of the original Surrency family beds passed down in the family. I will now recount the story as told by Madolyn Surrency Roberts.

Although many years have passed since the ghost invaded the house of the Surrency family at Surrency, Georgia, the mystery that surrounded the episode is as fascinating as ever. The unexplainable being appeared and manifested its presence in many ways, although it was never actually seen. Then it went away as suddenly and silently as it came.

I have taken the following account from the lips of members of the Surrency family and it is as accurate as can be after a lapse of so many years. Built among the pines of South Georgia is the small town of Surrency, situated on the Southern Railroad about 215 miles south of Atlanta.

About the year 1872, all this land was owned by Allan Surrency, who was the leading citizen of the town. He put up a large sawmill which was named for him, and operated a general store and a naval stores business. He owned several houses that he rented and a two-story dwelling in which he and his family lived. This dwelling was also known as the hotel and furnished accommodations for visitors to the village. Considering the value of property at that time, Mr.Surrency was a very rich man.

On the day of the ghost's first performances Mr. Surrency had gone to Macon to buy supplies for the store and hotel. That night one of the guests at the Surrency home was a minister, who was sitting in the room chatting with one of the older Surrency boys, when they heard a noise on the front porch. It sounded as if someone were throwing a heavy object against the door. The boy got up and went outside to investigate. Then he returned to the room he said that the noise was caused by bricks falling on the porch and that they were hot bricks.

Clem, a young married daughter, was visiting her parents and on the night of her arrival in Surrency her father was expected to return from Macon on the early night train. She walked out to the station to meet the train. When she reached the railroad tracks, she saw a bright light approaching. The light grew larger and brighter. Clem noticed it was not accompanied by the sound of a train. When the strange eerie light was almost upon her, she turned and ran as fast as she could for the house. Just as she entered the front door, she was followed by another shower of hot bricks.

As Clem was explaining about the weird light and the bricks, a number of things in the room began to fall. A whatnot stand in the corner toppled over, throwing all the china ornaments on the floor and smashing them into small bits. The minister we mentioned a little earlier threw a stick of wood on the fire. The stick immediately jumped out on the floor. The minister picked it up and replaced it on the fire, but the instant he released it the wood was back on the floor again. Then the tongs fell from their rack with a loud clatter and could not be made to stay in place on the rack.

A couple of smoothing irons jumped off a shelf, narrowly missing the minister's head. He sprang from his chair to dodge the smoothing irons, and just then the mantle clock began to strike. After striking several hundred times, it stopped and could not be made to run again. To make matters worse, the doors and windows refused to stay closed, so Mrs. Surrency called on the minister to help her. He stepped across the room to close one of the windows. He lowered the sash , but the moment he took his hands off, it flew up to the top again, then came down with a thunderous bang, shattering all the glass to bits.

The minister gave up on the window and walked over to the door, just as weird noises began to sound outside. He quickly closed the door and heard the latch click, but when he took his hand off the knob, the door was thrown open so violently that it swung against the wall and shook the whole house. This was repeated several times, although the key was turned in the lock. Finally the door was left open, although the weather was too cold to enjoy so much fresh air.

When Mr. Surrency arrived on the morning train, he found a large crowd gathered there to meet him and was told by several friends and neighbors that his house had been invaded by a haint! He hurried home and was followed by the train crew and all the passengers. Instead of the train remaining five minutes, it stayed one hour, while the train crew and passengers filled the house to see the strange doings.

When Mr. Surrency reached the house, he hurried in and asked his wife what it was all about. She explained the best she could, but her story was hardly necessary, for already the ghost was preparing a reception for him. Mr. Surrency, while in Macon, had bought some small articles for the home. Among them were nails and hooks for a clothes closet, and his first act on reaching home was to lock the articles in a dresser drawer in his bedroom. Then he returned to the yard to discuss the ghost with the crowd of neighbors gathered there. Glancing down, he found the nails and clothes hooks lying on the ground at his feet. As he stooped to pick them up, things began to happen.

The cordwood flew out of a rack nearby. Sticks of wood continued to fly through the air until the rack was entirely empty. Although several pieces came close to striking the scattering spectators, no one was injured.

On the morning following the first performance of the ghost, the Surrency family were sitting down to breakfast when the dishes suddenly dropped off the table and fell in a broken mass on the floor. When the cook attempted to put the food on the table, a dish of ham and a plate of biscuits went flying out the window. This trick was repeated many times in the days that followed.

The Surrency home, also called the hotel, was quite near and fronted the railroad, and was the home of relatives, friends, and passing visitors. It was a home full of kindness and hospitality. At first the family was amazed and dumbfounded by the goings on. They thought it possible that the tricks might have been perpetuated by someone in the family as a joke, or possibly by a neighbor or a little bit of fooling by some friend. Everyone who might have been guilty in the little town was checked up and accounted for. It didn't seem physically possible for anyone to do the strange things ascribed to the ghost. One morning while the old faithful cook , Sarah, was preparing breakfast the coffee pot, without any apparent cause, turned upside down on the stove. The cook placed a frying pan on the stove and filled it with slices of meat. She stepped to the table. When she turned back to the stove, the frying pan was upside down and the meat was sizzling on the fire. When she took the biscuits from the oven and set the pan on the table, the pan promptly sailed out of the window, throwing the biscuits on the ground. The pan fell with a loud bang on the steps. At times, the family was compelled to live on canned food for days, and even then they did not dare take their hands off the cheese and crackers or canned meat for fear the food would be smashed against the wall or go sailing out the window.

So many dishes were broken that Mr. Surrency bought tinware. It was nothing unusual for two or three garments to disappear during the night, often some of them never being seen again. A favorite prank of the ghost was to hide shoes or clothing in some corner where they would not be discovered until after the owner had worn himself out searching for them. One day Mr. Surrency took some of the things from the house and locked them in an outhouse to hide the articles from the ghost. Hardly had he put foot back in the house before the things were dumped on the floor behind him.

Among his possessions was an exceptionally handsome pair of cut glass wine decanters, presented to him by a hunting club of Savannah. Fearing they would be broken, he buried them in the garden. A few hours later, on going to the spot to see if they were safe, he found the decanters lying on top of the ground smashed into small bits. In three days time every piece of chinaware, glassware, and all the mirrors in the house were broken. For a while Mr. Surrency attempted to replace the glass as it was smashed, but he finally gave up in despair. Although the ghost seemed to delight in the destruction of property, it was never known to harm a person.

When the railroad was first built, all through the village, it was known as the East Tennessee. Then it was taken over by the Southern Railway. In those days locomotives burned wood instead of coal, and in front of the Surrency home was a rack always kept full of wood. Crossties to repair the tracks were piled along the right of way in front of the house. One day just as the passenger train stopped in front of the Surrency home, everyone left the train except the conductor and a friend, Captain Burns, who remained in one of the coaches. The windows of the coach were open and Captain Burns and his friend were sitting quietly chatting in one of the seats. To their horror, a huge crosstie whizzed through the window, narrowly missing Captain Burns' friend and passing through the opposite window, where it landed on the ground and stood upright like a fence post.

On another occasion, a young school teacher, a guest in the Surrency home, fearing the ghost would hide her shoes to embarrass her, tucked them under the mattress when she went to bed. On waking the next morning she looked for the shoes, but they were gone. A week or two later a cousin came to visit with the family and when she started to leave, her hat had disappeared. A few days after that a young man visiting the Surrency house came downstairs and announced that one of his rubber boots was missing. Some weeks later the teacher's shoes, the cousins hat, and the visitors boot were found again. They were lying in the center of one of the downstairs rooms, all in good condition. On another night as some of the boys were coming home, a shower of sticks, dead leaves, and trash fell over them. They thought that someone was trying to scare them and yelled out for the pranksters to stop getting their clothes dirty. Just then another shower of trash came down and they ran about among the trees and shrubbery looking for the source of the trash, but could find nothing. Next morning when they were seated at the breakfast table a shower of rice, cornmeal, sugar and some strange knives and forks they had never seen before, were dumped on the table. Books came out of the bookcases and fell on the floor. Empty chairs danced and moved about the room. Sticks and stones hopped about in the yard. Bricks would crash against the wall and fall to the floor. One uncomfortable thought was about the ghosts aim: suppose the bricks crashed against their heads instead of the wall!

Women guests were often afraid to sleep in their rooms alone. Sometimes several would share the same bedroom. Mattresses would be placed on the floor, but no sooner would the guests lie down than all of the chairs and some of the furniture in the room would pile on top of them. No one was hurt but they all agreed that it was not wise to sleep on the floor. On another occasion, hearing a strange noise in one of the bedrooms, they went to investigate and found the old-fashioned four poster bed dancing. It was nothing unusual to see thread, scissors, thimbles, or garments on which they had been working drifting through the air as though carried by an unseen hand. Pictures were snatched from the wall and hurled through the windows or doors. Sticks of wood were pitched out of the fire and onto the floor. On several occasions when the dishes were stacked in the pan for washing, the pan leaped to the floor with a bang, breaking the dishes into a thousand pieces.

The ghost delighted in mussing up newly made beds and more than once it caused food to disappear out of the frying pan. The cook stove cracked in many places, but continued cooking as well as when it was first bought. After smashing all the mirrors in the house, the ghost started on the win-dowpanes and did not rest until every pane was broken out. Quite often the feather beds, pillows, and mattresses would be jerked off the beds and pitched across the room. Chairs, even big rockers, were thrown across the rooms, some being slightly damaged and others broken to pieces.

One day Mrs. Surrency put a large ham in a big pot. She remained in the room until the ham was boiling; then to ensure its staying in the pot, she placed a heavy piece of iron over the lid. Leaving the kitchen, she walked to the front of the house. On entering the front room the first thing she saw was the ham lying on the hearth. She picked it up and ran with it back to the kitchen and found the pot of water still boiling. The ghost was not embarrassed by strangers and usually staged a performance especially for the visiting teachers. One day a minister arrived and after walking about the house and finding no signs of the ghost, said, "Well, it's just as I expect-ed—a fake, pure and simple." About this time a smoothing iron whizzed close by the preacher's ear and hit the wall with such force that it left a dent in the wood. A stick of wood fell from the ceiling, narrowly missing the preacher's head. With a gasp of amazement, he looked up to the ceiling to see where the wood came from, but finding no hole he rose from his chair and said, "seeing is believing, and now I think I will leave this town!"

Sticks of wood frequently fell by the side or in front of people as they walked about the rooms, even when the doors and windows were closed and there was no possibility of the wood being thrown from the outside. They would always look about to see if there was a hole in the wall or the ceiling, but there never was.

At first the Surrency family were frightened by the strange doings, but soon they became accustomed to the phenomena. But they had to admit it always gave them a start to watch the dishes rise from the table and fall in a broken mass on the floor, and it was not comfortable to have a brick whiz past your head and hit the wall.

One day as they sat at dinner two ears of corn dropped on the table. It was not like any corn grown by Mr. Surrency or anyone else in that part of the country. The next day Mrs. Surrency went upstairs. She noticed the floors were all wet as if they had just been scrubbed. While standing there, a shower of money fell at her feet and rolled about the floor. She picked it up and all who saw it agreed that it was coined many centuries past. Some days after this, a strange man came to the house and asked to be allowed to see the money. One of the younger boys of the family showed it to him and on some pretext the man sent the boy out of the room. When the boy returned, the man and the money had disappeared.

Finally driven to desperation by the ghosts weird pranks, the family moved from the big house and lived in a smaller one about five miles out in the country. But the ghost went with them and they soon returned to the big house. During a period of five years, thousands of people visited Surrency and the ghost. The railroad advertised its presence and ran special trains to carry visitors to the little town. The hospitality extended by Mr. Surrency during this time almost amounted to his ruin financially. No satisfactory explanation of the strange happenings in the Surrency home was ever offered. Scientists tried to solve the mystery but without success. It is estimated that 30,000 people visited the Surrency home while the ghost was active, but none of them could explain the queer The site of the ghost house and the surrounding property are still owned by a member of the Surrency family, but the old house was burned a few years ago and the ghost is now only a memory. But one that will never be forgotten.

Photo by Sandy Mudge

Chapter Twenty

Phantoms on Factors Walk

You don't have to walk very far in any direction in historic Savannah before encountering an area where there have been reports of paranormal activity. Just down from city hall eastward stands the old Cotton Exchange built in 1886. The Exchange is a long series of brick buildings that were used by the cotton merchants in Savannah to buy, sell, and trade what made the South King: Cotton! Millions of bales were shipped in and out of Savannah daily and was the key money crop of Georgia in the early nineteenth-century as well as rice and tobacco.

The Cotton Exchange buildings were divided by bays where the cotton was loaded and stored. The road directly in front of the Cotton Exchange is called Bay Street. It has been known for quite some time that the bays have many ghostly presences there. Many slaves that were brought to Savannah worked along River Street, loading cotton and doing heavy lifting and other dangerous tasks. The Cotton Exchange was built on the site of the earlier wooden warehouses that have long since burned down. The old warehouses were death traps to many of the slaves incarcerated in the holding pens.

Many of them fell ill and weren't cared for with the proper medicines and food. Those that rebelled against their masters were beaten and left locked up in several of the holding pens. If they murdered someone, they were often branded with an M on their foreheads. If a woman was raped and the slave was tried and found guilty, he was either hanged or burned at the stake at the town common which covered an area anywhere south of Oglethorpe Avenue. It was a very difficult life at best for a manual slave laborer at this point in Georgia's history.

I have written several reports before of people who have witnessed ghostly activity on River Street, Factors Walk, and Bay Street. This area has one of the deepest imprints from the past as anywhere else on this continent. Psychics who have researched the area all agree that a great deal of pain and suffering was meted out by cruel slave owners and others who took advantage of the oppressed slaves.

The Factors Walk phantoms in this true story are in the buildings currently numbered 208-220 East Bay Street. Several incidents have come to the forefront. Michael Fleetwood was kind enough to give me a tour of his office at 216 East Bay and fill me in on what he and two of the buildings tenants have seen. About five years ago Michael tells me he was photographing the outside of the buildings for an insurance policy and a strange blue anomaly appeared in the photograph at 208 East Bay Street. He has the photograph put away and told me he kept it because it was so strange. The tie with his photograph and what the lady in the office at 208 East Bay saw in her office collaborate one another's story. I walked next door and interviewed the tenant to affirm her side of this story.

The tenant tells me she came to work in the building on a Sunday morning to finish up some paper work from the week. She was sitting in her office and everything was still till she heard distinct footsteps just down the hall. She got up from her desk to see if there was anyone in the building but saw nothing. She went back to her desk and continued with her paperwork. She told me she never worked on Sundays and this was the first Sunday she ever went to work in the building. In the next few minutes on returning to her desk she told me she could feel a presence in the room with her. In this case she did not notice any change in the coolness of the air, but she knew someone was looking down on her and standing right beside her. She turned her head and saw a dark blue figure to her left. This was all the proof she needed that something was telling her to leave now and that she shouldn't be in the building working on a Sunday. It is unusual for someone to see a spirit directly head on. They are reported most of the time as being seen out of the corner of the eye. This spirit was pressing his point so she quickly got up, grabbed her purse, and exited the building. She has never gone back to the building on a Sunday or been in contact with the dark blue spirit since they last met.

A tenant on the other side who lives upstairs at # 220 hasn't noticed anything happening in her apartment, but she has friends who stay when she is out of town and they have had paranormal experiences. They reported noises, clanging, banging and a presence other than their own in the building.

Michael mentioned that a psychic came to investigate the buildings a while back and reported a black man in worker's overalls standing at the window and just staring out peacefully at the ships on the Savannah River. The psychic also told Michael that she could feel the presence of many children running from one end of the building to the other through the solid brick walls that separate the old bays. They use the buildings as their spiritual playground.

Photo by Sandy Mudge

Chapter Twenty One

The 1959 Harvey's Landing Train Wreck

So many tragedies have occurred where multiple lives have ended within the same few moments. Spirits passing all at once will stay together, at least in the first thirty to forty-five days according to some psychics and parapsychologists who study this phenomena. When the atomic bomb fell on Hiroshima, Japan, that fateful day in 1945, over 100,000 souls were annihilated within just a few seconds at ground point zero. These spirits' physical bodies were evaporated in the blink of an eye. The victims never realized the bright light they saw a split second before leaving their bodies was the flashpoint that touched off one of the most horrific weapons ever conceived in the mind of man, the atom bomb. One moment they were shopping in the markets and the next second, a crater the size equal to one caused by an impact with an asteroid a mile across is all that remained of their once illustrious city teeming with humanity. Their spirits never realized they had passed and continued their daily routines as if an explosion never occurred. The same theory holds true for crash victims in plane, automobile, ship and train disasters. This story is about a tragic train wreck that took place on a hot summer's day at Harvey's Landing, in Meldrim, Georgia, on Sunday, June 28th. 1959.

Harvey's Landing is located a short drive from Savannah to Meldrim, Georgia. Take I-16 West to Old River Road from downtown Savannah. The landing was a great spot for families to go to and swim in the cool waters of the Ogeechee River and picnic beside the Seaboard Railway train trestle that stretched to the opposite side. The 124 car Seaboard Airline Railway train that extended down the track for a mile was humming back towards Savannah with a large supply of natural gas tanks, and other flammable payloads. As the huge train was passing over the trestle, a large number of women and children were swimming and playing beneath the shadowy waters. One moment everything was peaceful and calm and in the next few moments lives would be engulfed in flames and burning debris as the couplings gave way on two monstrous freight cars and they leaped off the track directly at the innocent families enjoying a sunny afternoon down below. As one car followed another off the rail into the now murky waters two natural gas tankers ruptured and then exploded in heat so intense that all people near it were burned alive beyond recognition. The woods were on fire and the survivors were racing and swimming for cover as fast as they could but 20 unfortunate victims died there or in the days following the tragedy. All three of Savannah's hospitals, Chandler, Memorial, and St. Joseph's, were busy taking care of the burn victims and identifying the dead. The Georgia State Patrol, Chatham and Effingham County Police, The Navy, Marines, and The National Guard were all united to aid in the recovery of the living and to search out the remains of the dead. It was a terrible ordeal for all concerned to have to experience.

An official investigation was organized by the Interstate Commerce Commission who made their findings public information on September 3rd, 1959. The investigators found that the cause of the train's derailment was that excessive heat had caused the steel rails on the wooden trestle to expand. This upset the Seaboard Airline General Manager, Mr. J.N. Broetzman, who stated the tracks were built to expand with the temperature fluctuations and he stipulated a derailment such as this had never been attributed to temperature in the past.

Since this horrible tragedy took place, the Town of Meldrim dedicated Harvey's Landing as a Memorial Park in remembrance of that dreadful day over forty two years ago. I talked with the current owners Mr. and Mrs. William Burgess who tell me that today everything is quiet and peaceful there. So quiet and peaceful some say because the souls of those who died there are at peace and still swimming and picnicking on the other side.

Afterword

After gathering the last story for the final chapter of this, my second ghost and poltergeist-related book, I had to sit down and take a breather. There have been a number of stories of ghosts reported to the Searcherís paranormal research group recently. We have had so many calls lately for our investigations that there is now a backlog. First, we ask people who have a need of our free services to fill out a questionnaire. We ask simple questions about the type of haunting they may be experiencing and try to qualify each applicant on his or her own merit. We do our best to eliminate anything from our investigations that involves dementia or drugs and alcohol as the cause of that personís reported haunting. We have been good judges of human nature thus far in all the investigations the Searchers have handled. From what we learn in the questionnaire, we decide if their answers will warrant a site investigation. We will then make an appointment and bring our teams of researchers in to investigate and report back to the people living there our findings. We case file each of our investigations for future reference. These investigations have been intensely interesting and have opened many of our eyes and hearts to the spiritual world.

I speak for both my family and me when I say this work has made us all closer to our God in heaven. We have gone back to church and Sunday School on a regular basis. I now find a far deeper meaning to the Bible in my daily reading. I am discovering stories and passages that were drummed into me as a child in a whole new wonderful way!

Lila and the boys and I joined the Ardsley Park Baptist Church last year and have really enjoyed the services and warm openness of all the church members. Our church Pastor, Calvin Webb, is anointed in the word of God. I feel all the Sunday school teachers there are anointed as well.

I used to feel that people who claimed to be spiritual were just trying to draw attention to themselves. Now, I realize that being spiritual requires a great deal of maturity and faith.

I plan in the future to continue to investigate the strange and unusual in my hometown Savannah, Georgia, knowing full well I have a counterpart in every city throughout the United States. All of us have our own ghosts to investigate wherever humans have set foot and left an imprint on history and living. That is what makes this work of ghost research so much fun and educational to boot.

Author's Note

The characters in this book are real. Those who wished to remain anonymous I have made every effort to protect their right to privacy. The stories are all true and actually happened to the characters in each story. Many of these stories are taken (with kind permission) from actual case files of *The Searchers* in Savannah, Georgia.

I have been involved in many of the investigations presented in this book, and my intention throughout has been to remain faithful to the characters and events and to document them as they really happened.

AL COBB April 2001

Acknoulegments

I wish to express my heart-filled thanks to everyone who participated in supplying the true stories I have recounted in this book. The Savannahians who appear in these stories are all genuine as are their encounters with the unexplainable and the supernatural. I wish to thank all my fellow members of *The Searcher's*, a group of wonderful people interested in the paranormal and supernatural hauntings of Savannah, Georgia. They are Kathy Thomas (*Searcher's founder 1996*), Beth and Paul Ronberg (and their sons Jason and Noah), Billy and Caro Barrett, Jourdan Calderon, Sergio Calderon, Lynn Adams, Roger Arenas, Sandy and Kaya Mudge, my wife Lila and son's Jason and Lee Cobb, Rhonda McCall, Danny and Virgina Lamb, Janet Pence, Jennifer Johnson, Kathy Smith, Mark Stevens, Bobbie Weyl and her son Jason Weyl, and Alicia Willis.

In addition, a number of people in Savannah, who are not portrayed in these pages, were helpful to me in various ways: Jerry Fleming (Director City of Savannah Department of Cemeteries), The Georgia Historical Society for helping in our historical site research, and Burl Womack for his gift of the interview tape with Jim Williams.

Special thanks I give to Sandra Mudge, professional photographer and single mom who did a great job with her photography throughout this edition and Kathleen Thomas for her inside photographs and my photo on the back cover.

For his critical readings of my manuscript, I gratefully acknowledge my editor and friend David Norman, who teaches English at South College and Armstrong Atlantic State University in Savannah, Georgia.

Bibliography

Cobb, Al. Danny's Bed: A Tale of Ghosts and Poltergeists in Savannah, Georgia. Savannah, Georgia: Whitaker Street Press, 2000.

Feltman,Th.D., Melbourne I. The Holy Bible, Family Reading Edition, (King James). Chicago, Illinois: Consolidated Book Publishers, 1971.

Roberts, Madolyn Surrency. "The Ghost That Threw Bricks." in The Atlanta Journal Magazine. 15 Aug. 1940.

Map Key

1. Jeres Antiques
9 N. Jefferson St. Phantom spirits of children haunt the upstairs of the warehouse. (See Danny's Bed)

2. Factor's Walk
Site of cotton warehouses where slaves died and haunt the site. (See Savannah Ghosts)

3. River Street
The overall spiritual atmosphere is breath taking. There have been many reports of ghost activity. (See Savannah Ghosts)

4. 208-220 Bay Street
Many of ghost sightings have taken place here. Included are pirates, slaves, and clergymen. (See Savannah Specters, Savannah Ghosts, and Danny's Bed)

5. Trustee's Garden
18 E. Broad, next to the Pirates House, site of ghostly activity and strange occurrences in surrounding buildings and attached parking lot. (See Savannah Ghosts and Savannah Specters)

6. Pirates House
20 E. Broad. Famous restaurant with 200-year history of ghosts. (See Savannah Ghosts and Savannah Specters)

7. Hampton Lillibridge House
507 St. Julian Street. Site of an exorcism performed there in 1963 to rid the house of its entity. (See Savannah Ghosts and Savannah Specters)

8. Henry F. Willink House
426 St. Julian Street is haunted by Henry Willink, former shipbuilder for confederacy. (See Savannah Ghosts and Savannah Specters)

9. Mary Telfair Museum
121 Barnard St. has the ghost of Mary Telfair. (See Savannah Specters)

10. 300 West York Street
Several reports from this area include a male spirit walking down the street and a woman floating through a brick wall. (See Savannah Ghosts and Savannah Specters)

11. William H. Pinson House
Located at 304 E. State St. had ghostly and poltergeist activity reported in the past. (See Savannah Specters)

12. Juliette Gordon Low House
Girl Scout Headquarters at 10 E. Oglethorpe is Savannah's first National landmark. The ghosts of William and Nellie Gordon still haunt the home from time to time. (See Savannah Specters)

13. Juarez Restaurant
402 E. Broughton has a resident spirit of a female ghost. Customers and employees have seen her appear. (See Savannah Ghosts)

14. Marshall House Hotel
Site of Civil War hospital for Union soldiers occupying Savannah in 1864. Phantoms include a Union soldier, a young girl, and an alley cat. (See Savannah Ghosts)

15. St. John Episcopal Rectory
Once was the Green-Meldrim house. Haunted by the spirit of "Old Joe" a black butler who stays on duty every day. (See Danny's Bed and Savannah Specters)

16. Antique Alley
Located at 121 E. Gwinnett Street has the presence of a female spirit who misplaces items and then returns them. (See Danny's Bed)

17. Savannah Harley-Davidson Shop
Located at 503 East River Street. Employees experience the presence of a ghost. (See Savannah Ghosts)

18. Pink House Restaurant
23 Abercorn St. This famous restaurant is haunted by ghost of James Habersham, colonial settler and businessman. (See Savannah Ghosts and Savannah Specters)

19. Savannah Theatre
Located at 222 Bull St. This is the oldest theatre in America (1818). Sightings of apparitions upstairs in the balcony and projectionist room. (See Savannah Ghosts)

20. 1790 Restaurant
Located at 307 E. President has a resident ghost of a young girl named Anna who committed suicide there. (See Savannah Specters)

21. Owens Thomas House
124 Abercorn St. where many spirits have been seen in the garden and within the 200-year-old building. (See Savannah Specters)

22. Davenport House
324 E. State St. Haunted by a large, yellow spectral cat and other spirits. (See Savannah Specters)

23. The Kehoe House
123 Habersham St. This site has had multiple sightings of ghosts and phantom children. (See Savannah Ghosts)

24. Scarbrough House
Located at 41 Martin Luther King Blvd. Home of the "Rocking Chair Ghost" and other presences. (See Savannah Specters)

25. Forsyth Park
Once heavily wooded, the park was once used to bury many of the dead during the yellow fever epidemic of 1820. (See Savannah Ghosts)

26. 310 West Charlton
This house is believed to be haunted by Nicholas Curly who owned the building in the late 1840s. (See Savannah Specters)

27. 424 E. President Street
Reported in the past to have both ghostly and poltergeist activity. (See Savannah Specters)

28. 505 E. President Street
Former site of the Old Savannah Doll Museum had reports of a male spirit walking above the buildings occupants (See Savannah Specters)

29. 100 Block West Taylor Street
Several eyewitness accounts concerning ghostly presences and apparitions. (See Savannah Ghosts)

30. Old Female Orphanage Site
117 Houston Street. Two young girls who died in a fire in the early 19th century haunt the premises. (See Savannah Ghosts)

31. The Alexander Robert Lawton House
516 Abercorn Street. Ghost of General Lawton has been seen walking the halls.

32. Benjamin Wilson House
432 Abercorn St. There is a multitude of spirit activity including a poltergeist that frightened a family in 1973. (Danny's Bed)

33. 400 Block East Liberty & Price
A ghost of a young girl in a long white dress has been seen there in the past. (See Savannah Ghosts)

34. Piccadilly Restaurant
Located at 15 Bull St., former site of the Pulaski Hotel. Ghost of Gracie Watson haunts the site that was once her home. (Savannah Specters and Danny's Bed)

35. 400 Block of East Macon Street
A chill could be felt on the stairs from the presence of many unknown spirits. (Savannah Specters)

36. 400 Block East Gordon Street
Ghost of a young woman seen standing at the foot of a sleeping couples bed. (Savannah Specters)

37. Chippewa Square
Part of the 1779 site where the battle of Savannah was fought during the Revolutionary War. There is a great deal of spiritual activity here. (Savannah Specters)

38. Butler Mansion
622 Drayton St. Phantom apparitions of man dressed in Confederate uniform. (Savannah Specters)

39. Hamilton Turner Inn
330 Abercorn. The sounds of phantom children playing are often heard on the 3rd floor. (Savannah Specters)

40. Old Candler Hospital
Located on Gaston & Abercorn. Site of many supernatural events and haunted history dating back to the yellow fever epidemic in the early 19th century. (Savannah Specters)

41. Sarah E. Krenson House
Located at 214 W. Jones, tenants reported strong female spirit and sounds of light footsteps. (Savannah Specters)

42. 100 Block West Jones
Interesting paranormal reports has come from this row of houses which include poltergeist activity and cold spots. (Savannah Specters)

43. Colonial Cemetery
Located on Abercorn and Oglethorpe. Incredible spiritual place. (Savannah Ghosts and Savannah Specters)

44. 18 West Oglethorpe
Tenants have had very unusual contact with poltergeists. (Savannah Ghosts)

45. Krouskoff House
Located at 122 E. 37th Street and Abercorn, multiple ghost sightings and supernatural activities. (Savannah Ghosts)

46. Andrew Low House
Located at 329 Abercorn Street, reported sightings of female ghostly presence. (Savannah Specters)

Self-Guided Tour for Savannah's most haunted spots!

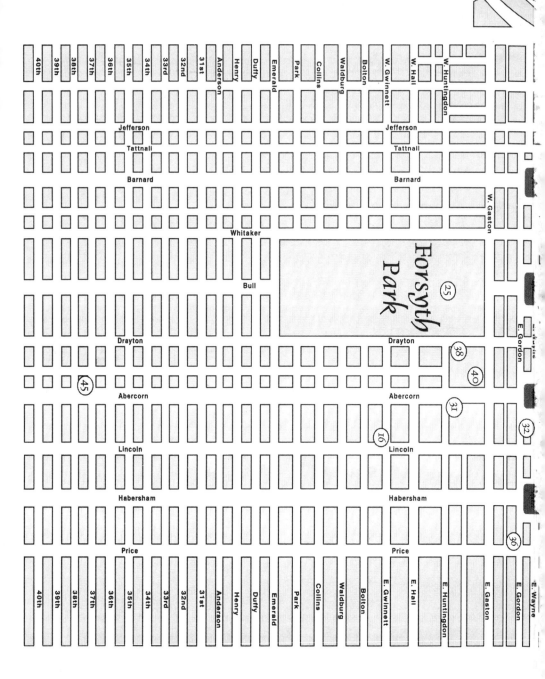